FOLLOWING JESUS

A DISCIPLE'S HANDBOOK

DALE EVRIST & JOEL EVRIST

CORE4
SERIES

TABLE OF CONTENTS

INTRODUCTION

In Jesus' earthly ministry He said and did everything according to the will of God the Father and the work of the Holy Spirit. He followed God's purposes and fulfilled God's plans in everything. He selected a group of men and called them to follow Him as He followed the Father in His plan to seek and to save the lost. In following Jesus, these men were spiritually transformed, becoming dynamic disciples capable of helping others to become followers and disciples of Him as well. They followed Jesus, were equipped by Him, imitated Him and shared His love and power with the world.

Following Jesus is a Bible-study handbook for everyone desiring to learn how to follow Jesus' example of obeying the will of God in everything by the truth of the Word and the power of the Holy Spirit. Then, to learn how to be a follower and disciple of Jesus Himself by imitating those who knew Him best, loved Him most and put Him first. Finally, to clearly see how the example of Jesus and His early followers give us a pattern to follow and a path to walk in our own pursuit of becoming dynamic disciples who help others to do the same.

In this resource, you will engage and go through 12 lessons that will help you learn how to follow Jesus and other faithful disciples in:

1. REPENTING AND BELIEVING

2. LOVING AND OBEYING

3. EMPOWERING AND LIBERATING

4. STUDYING AND APPLYING

5. PRAYING AND PRAISING

6. CONFESSING AND FORGIVING

7. WORSHIPING AND WORKING

8. EVANGELIZING AND DISCIPLING

9. RESISTING AND OVERCOMING

10. SERVING AND GIVING

11. SACRIFICING AND SUFFERING

12. RESTING AND ABIDING

In each lesson, you will find the following features to help guide you on your journey of becoming a more devoted disciple of the Lord Jesus:

Scriptures and Checkboxes

Following Jesus is filled with scriptures to be read and understood. The checkbox (❏) next to the reference is meant to be checked as each one is read. This will help you not to miss any of the biblical references as well as serve as an encouragement that you are familiarizing yourself with more and more of God's Word.

Lesson Introduction

Each lesson begins with some introductory thoughts on the lesson's theme. These will help you as a disciple to prepare your heart and mind to fully engage the subject matter.

Lesson Definition

There are clear and concise definitions of the words that make up the focus of each lesson and how they are used in the Bible. Understanding what these words mean in the languages the Scriptures were written will give you needed clarity for responding fully to the truths found in the lesson.

In the Life of Jesus

A major focus of *Following Jesus* is seeing, understanding and applying the principles and practices found in the life of Jesus in how He followed the will of the Father in everything. This is a unique feature of this resource and one that can have dynamic results in your life and the lives of those you guide through these lessons.

In the Lives of Jesus' Followers

Another major focus of *Following Jesus* is seeing, understanding and applying the principles and practices found in the lives of Jesus' early followers. These history-making Jesus-followers lived lives worth seeing clearly and imitating fully. This feature helps you do just that.

In Our Lives

Based upon a clear biblical study of how Jesus followed the will of the Father in everything and how His early disciples followed Jesus and His will in everything, this feature focuses on how we personally apply what has been observed and learned. The key to effectively using this resource is to clearly understand the path that Jesus and His followers pursued and to put their patterns of spiritual devotion into daily practice with the help of the Holy Spirit.

Memorize

As a part of each lesson, there is a scripture to memorize and meditate on. This will help the truths communicated to go deeper and be applied more dynamically in your life.

Key Truth

Much like the scripture to be memorized, there is a key truth that reinforces the primary focus of the lesson. This helps to more deeply "drive home" its theme.

Your Response

This part of each lesson helps you answer the "now what?" question. Here you will find steps of practical application that will make following Jesus as a devoted disciple an encouraging, enriching and effective reality.

Written Response: Lesson Review

By writing out certain parts of each lesson, you will be helped to review key sentences and statements and to reinforce their truths in your life.

Written Response: Life Reflection

This part of each lesson will help you to reflect on what you have learned and how you will apply that in your life. You will be provided prompts to help journal your journey as a growing disciple of Jesus.

GOING THROUGH FOLLOWING JESUS

You certainly can go through *Following Jesus* on your own and gain significant growth in your pursuit of knowing and serving the Lord Jesus. However, the most effective way to use this resource is to be guided through the process by another disciple who is more mature in following Jesus than you are. Thoroughly working through the lesson on your own and then having a regular discipleship meeting with someone committed to making disciples will produce even deeper and more dynamic results.

TAKING SOMEONE THROUGH FOLLOWING JESUS

After going through Following Jesus yourself, you will be ready to make an ongoing commitment to take others through this resource as well. If seeing *souls saved and disciples made* is to be our main priority and purpose in this life, then we need to engage this passion and practice regularly. Ask the Holy Spirit to lead you to those whom the Lord has called you to help become devoted disciples of Him. Set up regular discipleship meetings and have those you are discipling come into those meetings having thoroughly gone through the lesson you are covering. Your preparation will be reviewing the lesson, having prayed for the discipleship meeting and trusting the Holy Spirit to guide and grace every part.

The most important and most satisfying work you will ever do is helping people of all ages and stages to become faithful and fruitful followers of Jesus.

Lesson 1

———

FOLLOWING JESUS IN REPENTING AND BELIEVING

REPENTING AND BELIEVING INTRODUCTION

❏ *Read Mark 1:14-15*

Sometime after John the Baptist was thrown into prison for confronting the immorality of King Herod, Jesus picked up John's clear call to turn from sin and self to serve the living God through repenting, believing, and obeying. Jesus declared that if one was to enter the kingdom of God (God's royal and righteous rule), they had to repent and believe in the gospel (the good news that God the Father sent His Son into the world to save all who would humbly turn to God and trust the sacrifice of Jesus the Savior and Son). Jesus' call to repent and believe was unmistakable and unapologetic. He made it clear that it was absolutely necessary in order to pass from death into life and from darkness into light.

Jesus later confronted unrepentant and unbelieving religious leaders who had witnessed the repenting and believing of the worst sinners of the day—tax collectors and prostitutes. Yet the religious leaders, in their pride and self-righteousness, would not repent and would not believe. (❏ Read Matthew 21:28-32.) Jesus' desire was that

... He made it clear that the key that opened the door to God's grace and goodness was repenting and believing.

8

all men would receive the love, light, and life that His Father sent Him to provide in abundance. The Father loved the world and sent His Son to tell them of His great passion and purpose to open the door of salvation and deep satisfaction of soul. (❑ Read John 3:13-17.) But He made it clear that the key that opened the door to God's grace and goodness was repenting and believing.

REPENTING AND BELIEVING DEFINED

Repenting involves turning away from something and turning toward something else. As a disciple, repenting is turning away from anything that does not line up with God's Word, will, and ways as expressed perfectly in the example of Jesus and turning toward everything that does. In the Bible, repenting means a change of heart that results in a change of decision and direction. It means different thinking on a matter that produces different attitudes and actions. Genuine repenting involves intellect, emotion, and will—thinking, feeling, and doing.

Genuine repenting involves intellect, emotion, and will—thinking, feeling, and doing.

Genuine believing is a conviction that produces a corresponding conduct.

Believing involves relying completely on something or someone in unwavering confidence. As a disciple, believing is being fully focused on the person, promises, and power of God the Father and Jesus the Son as revealed in the Word of God. Throughout the Scriptures, believing means to place confidence in or to trust completely. The ultimate indicator of what we believe is how we behave. We will always act on what we truly believe. Genuine believing is a conviction that produces a corresponding conduct.

REPENTING AND BELIEVING IN THE LIFE OF JESUS

While Jesus had nothing to repent of, He went everywhere calling men to repent. Jesus called people to turn from sin and self, from false and fleshly thinking, and put their faith in Him—the only source of truth and spiritual transformation. He called and challenged people to do away with foolish notions that were contrary to God's Word, will, and ways. He exposed religious hypocrites and called people to turn from the destructive influence in their lives and to look to the God of grace, love, and mercy who sent His Son to help them find their way to Him. (❏ Read Luke 5:29-32.)

Jesus believed completely in the mission His Father had given Him. This was a mission to seek and save and rescue and redeem lost and broken humanity. He believed absolutely in the power of the Holy Spirit to anoint and empower Him to speak and to act according to the perfect will of the Father. This included defeating the devil and his demonic kingdom of darkness and establishing His kingdom in the hearts of all who would repent and believe on Him. (❏ Read Luke 4:14-21.)

REPENTING AND BELIEVING IN THE LIVES OF JESUS' FOLLOWERS

Jesus' followers first engaged Him by repenting and believing. Some of them had initially been disciples of John the Baptist, as they responded to his message to repent and believe that Messiah and His kingdom were coming. (❏ Read John 1:35-37.) So, when they heard Jesus issuing the same call, they recognized their need to respond to Him. (❏ Read Matthew 4:17-20.) This began an ongoing journey of discovering their need to repent of wrong thinking, attitudes, and actions and to be conformed more and more to the message and ministry of Jesus. They discovered that repenting and believing was an ongoing process rather than just a single act. As followers of Jesus, they learned increasingly how to conform their thinking, believing, and behaving in a manner consistent with His mission, message, and ministry. (❏ John 13:12-17.)

After the crucifixion, resurrection, and ascension of Jesus, the disciples went everywhere preaching and teaching a message of repenting and believing. (❏ Read Acts 2:38-39; 3:18-21; 8:35-37.) They also continued in a lifestyle

Notes

Notes

of repenting and believing. Simon Peter needed the Spirit to give him clarity on the fact that Jesus died to make Jew and Gentile equal in every way and that the grace of God, apart from the law, would save them and receive them fully through repenting and believing. (❏ Read Acts 10.) There was also a council of church leaders who came together in Jerusalem to debate what requirements should be placed on Gentile believers. After much discussion, debate, and deliberation in the presence of the Lord, the Holy Spirit spoke, challenging and changing their thinking and believing. They responded to the Spirit's wisdom and revelation with actions that indicated real repenting and believing had taken place. (❏ Read Acts 15:1-32.) The Apostle Paul taught consistently on the need for repenting and believing in his letters to the churches. (❏ Read Romans 2:4; 2 Corinthians 7:9-10.)

REPENTING AND BELIEVING IN OUR LIVES

Repenting and believing is how we are saved and enter the kingdom of God. (❏ Read Mark 1:14-15.) And repenting and believing is how we continue to see the work of salvation and the rule of King Jesus increase in our lives. If repenting is turning away from anything that does not line up with God's Word, will, and ways, it means that we must be open to ongoing changes of heart and mind that result in changes in beliefs and behaviors, attitudes and actions. (❏ Read Ephesians 4:20-24.) Repenting as a lifestyle requires personal revelation and personal response. This is what the Holy Spirit desires to lead us in each and every day. (❏ Read Romans 8:13-14.)

One of the main issues in a Christian's life is how we think and what we believe.

If believing involves relying completely on something or someone in unwavering confidence, then it is absolutely necessary for us to grow in being more and more focused on the person, promises, and power of Jesus. Faith is like a muscle—the more it is exercised, the more it grows. The more we choose to believe the Word of God, the more we will behave according to the Word of God. This is how we grow in grace and the true knowledge of our Lord and Savior Jesus Christ. (❏ Read 2 Peter 3:18.) One of the main issues in a Christian's life is how we think and what we believe. Healthy and sound thinking and believing will produce healthy and sound emotions and feelings. (❏ Read Philippians 4:8-9.)

Notes

MEMORIZE: *"Now after John was put in prison, Jesus came to Galilee, preaching the gospel of the kingdom of God, and saying, 'The time is fulfilled, and the kingdom of God is at hand. Repent, and believe in the gospel.'"* (Mark 1:14-15)

Use the following lines to write out the scripture to help you commit it to memory.

_____

_____

_____

_____

_____

_____

_____

KEY TRUTH: Jesus' call to repent was unmistakable and unapologetic. He made it clear that it was absolutely necessary in order to pass from death into life and from darkness into light.

YOUR RESPONSE:

This is how you can respond in loving obedience to Jesus as you apply the truths from this lesson to your life.

- Ask the Holy Spirit to reveal places in your life where you need to repent of sin and self and confess those to God, believing in His ability to renew your mind and refresh your heart.

- Make a daily commitment to allow your thinking to be adjusted to better line up with God's Word, will and ways.

- Pay attention to areas where your confession does not line up with your conduct and make a fresh commitment to believe God's Word and act accordingly.

- Meditate on the promises in God's Word to bless your life abundantly believing fully that they will come to pass.

WRITTEN RESPONSE: LESSON REVIEW

Review each section from the lesson on the previous pages to fill in each blank below. This review will help to reinforce the truths from this lesson in your life.

1. _____ involves _____
    _____ from something and _____
    _____ something else.

2. _____ involves _____ _____ on
    something or someone in _____ _____.

3. Jesus called people to _____ from
    _____ and _____, from
    _____ and _____ thinking, and put
    their _____ in Him—the only _____
    of _____ and spiritual _____.

4. After the crucifixion, resurrection, and ascension
    of Jesus, the _____ went everywhere
    _____ and _____ a _____
    of _____ and _____.

5. _____ and _____ is how we are
    _____ and _____ the kingdom of God.

WRITTEN RESPONSE: LIFE REFLECTION

Using the journaling section on the pages at the end of this lesson, write in your own words your responses to the following questions.

1. What have you learned and what has impacted you personally from this lesson?

2. In reading the scripture references in this lesson, what are you sensing and seeing the Holy Spirit highlighting and revealing to you that will enable you to better follow Jesus?

3. As a disciple and follower of Jesus, what steps of loving obedience do you need to take to see what you have learned in this lesson become ongoing practices and patterns in your life?

Journal

Journal

—

FOLLOWING JESUS IN LOVING AND OBEYING

LOVING AND OBEYING INTRODUCTION

❏ *Read John 14:21-24*

"If anyone loves Me, he will keep my word." These words, from the mouth of Jesus, have powerfully echoed through the ages in the hearts of disciples who long to follow their Master and fulfill His divine purposes for their lives. Jesus emphasized that loving and obeying are two sides of the same coin. Those who love the Lord Jesus obey the Lord Jesus. In His Great and Supreme Commission, Jesus charged His followers to make disciples by teaching them to observe (obey) all things He commanded. (❏ Read Matthew 28:18-20.)

The example they were following was His, for Jesus had modeled beautifully how to love and obey by the way He had loved and obeyed His Heavenly Father. His pursuit became their passion in loving and obeying their Lord. The same Lord calls us to love Him by obeying Him today in like manner.

> *Those who love the Lord Jesus obey the Lord Jesus.*

LOVING AND OBEYING DEFINED

Understanding *love* in its purest form is only found in the character of God, which we find in the Word of God.

The New Testament's primary word for love is agape (ah-gah-pay), which describes the Father's love for the world, Christ's love for His followers, and the kind of love Christ demands for Himself and others. This kind of love isn't focused on what it can get, but what it can give. This love does whatever it takes for as long as it takes for the benefit of the one being loved. This love flows from a divine source in our lives: The Holy Spirit. (❑ Read Galatians 5:22.) When we come into Christ Jesus by faith, we are born again into God's family, and the Holy Spirit dwells within us, supplying us with this divine love. As we walk by (remain in, live in, abide in) the Holy Spirit, this divine love that we have received from the Father through the Son is readily available to richly release back to our Lord and those around us.

This love does whatever it takes for as long as it takes for the benefit of the one being loved.

The words for *obedience* in the New Testament have mostly to do with intently listening to a command, vigorously protecting what's been said, and thoroughly carrying out the command to completion. The writers of the New Testament considered being a servant and follower of Jesus to be their highest and most cherished honor. In their minds, it was inconceivable to claim to love Jesus without diligently obeying Him. Precise and particular

Notes

attention to the details of Christ's demands were seen as the mandate and mission of every devoted disciple of the Lord Jesus. (❏ Read Romans 1:1-7; Jude 1-2.)

LOVING AND OBEYING IN THE LIFE OF JESUS

Jesus said that He only did what He saw the Father doing and only said what He heard the Father saying. (❏ Read John 5:19; 12:50.) He did this because He loved the Father and sought to meticulously obey Him in every word and deed. Jesus told His disciples that they were to constantly remain in His love as He had remained in the love of the Father. He told them that He remained in the Father's love by keeping all of His Father's commandments, and they would remain in His love by keeping His. (❏ Read John 15:9-10.) This is how Jesus so steadily received and reciprocated God's awesome love. In these scriptures, Jesus uses the word "kept" to describe His complete obedience. The word *kept* means to attend to carefully, take care of, guard, pay special attention to, watch over, and hold fast to something. Jesus faithfully loved His Heavenly Father by faithfully obeying His Father's commandments in everything.

> *Jesus faithfully loved His Heavenly Father by faithfully obeying His Father's commandments in everything.*

LOVING AND OBEYING
IN THE LIVES OF JESUS' FOLLOWERS

As stated earlier, Jesus left His disciples a Great and Supreme Commission to make disciples by teaching them to observe (keep, guard, and obey) His commandments.

> *Loving and obeying Jesus is voluntary, but never optional for the true disciple.*

The early church and New Testament writers lovingly followed Jesus' example of loving obedience to the Father. Jesus' early disciples were obedient to the apostles' teaching about Jesus.

(❏ Read Acts 2:42.) Peter and John were obedient in the face of persecution. (❏ Read Acts 4:19-20; 5:28-29.) The Apostle Peter was obedient to the vision Jesus showed him and the leading of the Holy Spirit to Cornelius' house. (❏ Read Acts 10:1-48.) Jesus showed Paul a vision for his calling and Paul thoroughly obeyed. (❏ Read Acts 26:12-19.) The church at Rome was called to follow the example of the loving obedience of Jesus. (❏ Read Romans 5:19; 6:17.) The writer of Hebrews, the Apostle Peter, and the Apostle James all joyfully called disciples of Jesus to follow Christ's example of loving obedience and to be diligent doers of His Word. (❏ Read Hebrews 5:8; James 1:22-25; 1 Peter 1:2.)

In all of these examples, we see Jesus' disciples understanding the principle and power of loving and obeying through an abiding devotion to the will and work of Jesus. Loving and obeying Jesus is voluntary, but never optional for the true disciple. For only in loving and obeying King Jesus is His kingdom rule released and established in the earth.

LOVING AND OBEYING IN OUR LIVES

Jesus, the King of all kings and the Lord of all lords, the very Ruler of the universe, offers intimate friendship to any and all. The key to this friendship is simple and yet profound: believe Him, love Him, and obey Him in everything. (❏ Read John 15:9-14.) This is our passion, this is our pursuit, this is our prize. But this can never be achieved by our own work or our own wisdom. This must come by the truth of God's Word and the work of God's Spirit in our hearts and lives.

> *... believe Him, love Him, and obey Him in everything.*

As disciples of Jesus we must allow His Holy Spirit to empower and guide us into the same life of loving obedience that Jesus embodied and exemplified while here on earth. The endless supply of God's love in Christ Jesus is ours for the receiving as we open every corner of our life to the Spirit's work. It is in this and this alone that a life of loving and obeying can be firmly established and deeply enjoyed.

MEMORIZE: *"He who has My commandments and keeps them, it is he who loves Me. And he who loves Me will be loved by My Father, and I will love him and manifest Myself to him."* (John 14:21)

Use the following lines to write out the scripture to help you commit it to memory.

_____

_____

_____

_____

_____

_____

_____

KEY TRUTH: As disciples of Jesus we must allow His Holy Spirit to empower and guide us into the same life of loving obedience that Jesus embodied and exemplified while here on earth.

YOUR RESPONSE:

This is how you can respond in loving obedience to Jesus as you apply the truths from this lesson to your life.

- As you daily study the Word, ask the Holy Spirit to show you Christ's commands.

- Ask in faith for Jesus to give you fresh daily fillings of the Holy Spirit. Ask the Spirit to provide you with the knowledge of what you must lovingly obey, the wisdom concerning how to lovingly obey, and the power and endurance to lovingly obey.

- Make repentance for disobedience a constant practice. Ask the Holy Spirit to show you any attitudes and actions that "fall short" of loving obedience. Confess, repent, receive forgiveness, and freshly commit to loving and obeying Jesus.

- Actively seek to learn from those who lovingly obey Jesus more than you do. Ask questions. To the degree they imitate Christ, imitate them.

WRITTEN RESPONSE: LESSON REVIEW

Review each section from the lesson on the previous pages to fill in each blank below. This review will help to reinforce the truths from this lesson in your life.

1. The New Testament's primary word for _____
    is _____, which describes the Father's
    love for the _____, Christ's love for His
    _____, and the kind of love Christ _____
    for _____ and _____ .

2. The words for _____ in the New Testament
    have mostly to do with _____ _____
    to a command, _____ _____
    what's been said, and _____ _____
    out the command to _____.

3. Jesus _____ loved His Heavenly Father
    by _____ _____ His Father's
    _____ in _____.

4. _____ and _____ Jesus is voluntary,
    but never _____ for the true _____.

5. As _____ of Jesus we must allow His Holy Spirit
    to _____ and _____ us into the
    same life of _____ _____ that Jesus
    _____ and _____ while here on earth.

WRITTEN RESPONSE: LIFE REFLECTION

Using the journaling section on the pages at the end of this lesson, write in your own words your responses to the following questions.

1. What have you learned and what has impacted you personally from this lesson?

2. In reading the scripture references in this lesson, what are you sensing and seeing the Holy Spirit highlighting and revealing to you that will enable you to better follow Jesus?

3. As a disciple and follower of Jesus, what steps of loving obedience do you need to take to see what you have learned in this lesson become ongoing practices and patterns in your life?

Journal

Journal

Lesson 3

———

FOLLOWING JESUS IN EMPOWERING AND LIBERATING

EMPOWERING AND LIBERATING INTRODUCTION

❏ *Read Luke 4*

After Jesus was baptized in water by John the Baptist and baptized and filled with the Holy Spirit by Father God, He immediately moved into the wilderness of Judea where He was tempted by the devil, but resisted and overcame him in every possible way. After that, He went up to His hometown of Nazareth where He announced that Isaiah's prophecy of an anointed and appointed Messiah coming to empower and liberate bound and broken mankind had been fulfilled in Him.

During this time, Jesus began His mission and ministry through the power of the Holy Spirit. This included preaching the good news of salvation, healing the sick and afflicted, and delivering those demonically harassed and oppressed. He preached that the kingdom, or royal rule of the God of heaven, had come to bring power to the powerless and liberty to those lost and locked up in a prison of pain and hopelessness. He came as the empowered liberator to set people free from

He came as the empowered liberator to set people free from the penalty and power of sin, and to send them on a mission of doing the same for everyone, everywhere.

36

the penalty and power of sin, and to send them on a
mission of doing the same for everyone, everywhere.

EMPOWERING AND LIBERATING DEFINED

Empowering must be something received and released. To
be empowered one must be saved, baptized and filled by
the power of the Holy Spirit through the person of Jesus.
Having received the power of God—His supernatural
strength to save and set free—one is sent to bring
that same freedom into the lives of others. The word
empowering in the New Testament has to do with Jesus
sharing His divine ability to rescue, redeem and restore.

Likewise, *liberating* is something received and released.
To be liberated means that one has been set free from
the impact of sin and the influence of satanic forces.
Having been liberated by the truth of the gospel of grace
in Christ Jesus and the transformational power of the Holy Spirit, one then brings that same liberation into the lives of others. Anointed by Jesus, the Liberator, one is then appointed to use His name and authority to set the captives free.

> *Empowering must be something received and released.*

> *Likewise, liberating is something received and released.*

Notes (❏ Read Isaiah 61:1; Luke 4:18-19.) The word *liberating* in the Bible has to do with setting men free from the ravages of sin by the redemptive power of God in Christ Jesus.

EMPOWERING AND LIBERATING IN THE LIFE OF JESUS

Everywhere Jesus went, He brought divine power and liberty. The Apostle Peter, in his message to those in Cornelius' house, summed up Jesus' ministry as one of helping and healing people, setting them free from demonic influence by the power of God. (❏ Read Acts 10:38.) He was anointed for the ministry of empowering and liberating everyone who would receive Him and believe in Him. (❏ Read John 1:12-13.) As Jesus announced that the kingdom of God had come, miracles and manifestations of God's love and power broke in on the earthly scene and the human condition. (❏ Read Matthew 12:22-29.)

Every word Jesus spoke was attested to by the work of the Holy Spirit's power, authenticating His message and ministry, empowering and liberating people everywhere.

It was the mission of Jesus to manifest the Father's love and mercy in bringing people out of bondage and into the blessing of new birth. (❑ Read John 3:5-8, 12-17.) Every word Jesus spoke was attested to by the work of the Holy Spirit's power, authenticating His message and ministry, empowering and liberating people everywhere. (❑ Read Luke 7:22.)

EMPOWERING AND LIBERATING IN THE LIVES OF JESUS' FOLLOWERS

What Jesus did in ministering fullness and freedom to all He encountered became a model for those who followed Him. He sent His twelve disciples out with delegated authority and divine power to bring spiritual life and liberty to the people of every city they entered. He commissioned them to declare and demonstrate the passion and power of the Father to all. (❑ Read Luke 9:1-6.) He then sent scores of other followers into other cities to prepare the way for His coming by preaching the King and the kingdom, and healing and delivering all who had need. (❑ Read Luke 10:1-9.)

After Jesus' death and resurrection, He instructed His disciples to wait together in Jerusalem until they were clothed with the power of the Holy Spirit, anointing them to be authentic witnesses for Him. (❑ Read Matthew 28:18-20; Mark 16:15-20; Luke 24:46-49.) They did just that. On the Day of Pentecost they were marvelously filled to bring fullness and freedom to all. (❑ Read Acts 2:1-42.) What they received from heaven above, they released

Notes

Notes

on earth below. The Anointed One, Jesus, had now empowered a liberating force of anointed ones who could freely give to others what had freely been given to them.

Throughout the Book of Acts, we see Jesus' disciples continuing to minister spiritual fullness and freedom. (❑ Read Acts 5:12-16; 8:4-7; 10:44-48; 16:25-34; 19:1-10.) Throughout the epistles, the Lord's disciples wrote to instruct and remind believers that this ministry of empowering and liberating that had impacted them was to be imparted to others. (❑ Read Romans 13:7-13; 2 Corinthians 5:17-21; Ephesians 6:10-20; 1 Peter 2:4-10.) What began on the day of Pentecost was to be shared with all people of every generation. (❑ Read Acts 2:38-39.)

EMPOWERING AND LIBERATING IN OUR LIVES

As followers of Jesus and devoted disciples, we are called to receive the empowering and liberating work of the Holy Spirit and then to release the ministry of empowering and liberating into the lives of others. Because we are in Christ and Christ is in us, we can carry His fullness and freedom wherever we go. We are an anointed and appointed people who are to

> *Because we are in Christ and Christ is in us, we can carry His fullness and freedom wherever we go.*

continue all that Jesus began to do and teach when He was on the earth. (❏ Read Acts 1:1-3.)

This means that as Jesus and His followers preached the gospel with truth and liberating power, we do the same. This means that as Jesus and His followers lived and worked by the power of the Holy Spirit in everything with everyone, we do the same. This means that as Jesus and His followers dealt with demonic forces and set people free by His divine authority, we do the same. And this means that as Jesus and His followers lived daily as witnesses of the will of the Father to save and set free, we do the same. (❏ Read Acts 1:8.)

Notes

MEMORIZE: *"The Spirit of the LORD is upon Me, because He has anointed Me to preach the gospel to the poor; He has sent Me to heal the brokenhearted, to proclaim liberty to the captives and recovery of sight to the blind, to set at liberty those who are oppressed; to proclaim the acceptable year of the LORD."* (Luke 4:18-19)

Use the following lines to write out the scripture to help you commit it to memory.

_____

_____

_____

_____

_____

_____

_____

KEY TRUTH: It was the mission of Jesus to manifest the Father's love and mercy in bringing people out of bondage and into the blessing of new birth.

YOUR RESPONSE:

This is how you can respond in loving obedience to Jesus as you apply the truths from this lesson to your life.

- If you have yet to be baptized and filled with the person and power of the Holy Spirit, seek someone to agree in prayer with you to fully receive Christ's empowering. If you have been baptized and filled, seek to walk in the Holy Spirit's power, releasing empowering to others every day.

- Ask the Spirit to reveal to you the areas in your life where you have been liberated and set free from sinful strongholds and areas where you have not.

- Seek someone to agree in prayer with you to fully receive Christ's liberating work. Then seek to release the liberating power of Christ into the lives of others.

- Confess daily that you have been anointed by the Anointed One to follow Him in empowering and liberating every life you touch.

WRITTEN RESPONSE: LESSON REVIEW

Review each section from the lesson on the previous pages to fill in each blank below. This review will help to reinforce the truths from this lesson in your life.

1. _____ must be something
   _____ and _____.

2. To be _____ means that one has been
   set _____ from the _____ of
   sin and the _____ of satanic forces.

3. Every _____ Jesus spoke was _____ to
   by the _____ of the Holy Spirit's _____,
   authenticating His _____ and _____,
   _____ and _____ people everywhere .

4. What Jesus did in _____ _____ and
   _____ to all He _____ became a
   _____ for those who _____ Him .

5. As _____ of Jesus and _____
   _____, we are called to _____ the
   _____ and _____ work of the Holy Spirit
   and then to _____ the ministry of _____
   and _____ into the lives of _____.

WRITTEN RESPONSE: LIFE REFLECTION

Using the journaling section on the pages at the end of this lesson,
write in your own words your responses to the following questions.

1. What have you learned and what has impacted you personally
    from this lesson?

2. In reading the scripture references in this lesson, what are you
    sensing and seeing the Holy Spirit highlighting and revealing to
    you that will enable you to better follow Jesus?

3. As a disciple and follower of Jesus, what steps of loving
    obedience do you need to take to see what you have learned in
    this lesson become ongoing practices and patterns in your life?

Journal

Journal

FOLLOWING JESUS IN STUDYING AND APPLYING

STUDYING AND APPLYING
INTRODUCTION

❏ *Read Matthew 22:37-38; Psalm 119:1-2*

A disciple of Jesus is to be a life-long learner and doer of truth. Jesus said that the greatest commandment was to love God with all of one's heart, soul, and mind (thinking, desiring, and understanding). (❏ Read Matthew 22:34-37; Mark 12:28-30.) Part of the purpose for God's design of the mind is for studying and applying. The Word of God reveals that man has been created to search out God's truth in investigation, meditation and application. (❏ Read Proverbs 25:2; Psalm 111:2.) People were created by God to pursue Him in order to understand His Word, will and ways.

Throughout the Scriptures we are commissioned to diligently study and thoroughly apply the truth of God's Word. (❏ Read Proverbs 1:5; 1 Corinthians 2:9-12.) Studying and applying become a dynamic source of deep satisfaction because they represent the passionate pursuit of knowing God as Creator and King.

> *Throughout the Scriptures we are commissioned to diligently study and thoroughly apply the truth of God's Word.*

STUDYING AND APPLYING DEFINED

In the Scriptures, *studying* means thoroughly investigating and inquiring into something with the intent of discovering it's true meaning and value. It's like mining for jewels with a refusal to quit until you find what you're looking for. We are commanded to diligently study the Word and works of God to thoroughly understand what God does, with the desire and devotion to do the same. (❏ Read Psalm 111:1-10.) And, we not only study to thoroughly understand what God does, but also who He is. (❏ Read Proverbs 8:1-17.) The writer of Hebrews tells us that we are to grow in faith as we diligently seek the knowledge of God. (❏ Read Hebrews 11:6.) The term *diligently seek* means to investigate, scrutinize, inquire about, and ardently crave something. This is what God wants us to do with Him. He is well pleased with our faithful study of who He is, and He promises to reward us accordingly. His rewards include revelation of Him and the knowledge, wisdom, and understanding to obey Him and become more like Him. As disciples of Jesus, we are called to a lifelong study of who God is, what He has done, and what He plans to do. To study the Word of God is to study the God of the Word.

In the Scriptures, *applying* means putting into action what is revealed and required. It means that what has been thoroughly studied must be steadfastly applied. Jesus said that once something was known it had to be acted upon to access and appropriate God's blessings. (❏ Read

Matthew 7:24-28; John 13:17.) It's only when information becomes application that it turns into revelation and leads to transformation. To truly know God,

> *To truly know God, there must be diligent studying and devoted applying of the righteous requirements of God's Word.*

there must be diligent studying and devoted applying of the righteous requirements of God's Word.

STUDYING AND APPLYING IN THE LIFE OF JESUS

No one has ever exemplified studying and applying better than Jesus. He is without a doubt history's greatest biblical scholar and practitioner. From His youth, He was found diligently studying and applying truth. He astonished the teachers of His day with His understanding of the Scriptures. (❏ Read Luke 2:46-49.) He was hungry for the truth and how to apply it. During His public ministry, the people of Israel were amazed by His understanding, teaching, and practical application of truth though he had no formal education as a rabbi. Jesus made it clear to them that His doctrine (His teachings and practices) were given

> *No one has ever exemplified studying and applying better than Jesus.*

to Him by His Heavenly Father whom He had diligently sought in the Word and by the Spirit. (❑ Read John 7:15-18.) Jesus memorized and meditated on vast amounts of Scripture, meticulously applying all that He had diligently studied. (❑ Read Matthew 5:17.) Through all of Jesus' studying and applying, there came the obeying and fulfilling of all that God had commanded and all that God had promised. (❑ Read Matthew 8:16-17.)

STUDYING AND APPLYING IN THE LIVES OF JESUS' FOLLOWERS

Jesus told His disciples that powerful signs and wonders would result from their commitment to the message of the gospel and the mission of seeing souls saved and disciples made. (❑ Read Mark 16:15-20.) His disciples immediately applied this truth by speaking the words and doing the works of Jesus believing Him and obeying Him in everything. Jesus had opened His disciples' understanding to comprehend what the Scriptures said concerning the Christ, and His disciples boldly proclaimed and thoroughly taught what Jesus had taught them. (❑ Read Luke 24:45; Acts 2:42; 5:42; 6:4.) In order for someone to be qualified for any significant leadership role in the church, they had to know and be able to apply the Scriptures. (❑ Read Acts 6:3-7.) When Christians were forced to leave Jerusalem due to persecution, they effectively preached the Word of God everywhere they went. (❑ Read Acts 8:4.) Philip, Peter, and John preached the doctrine of Christ and the

baptism with the Holy Spirit to the Samaritans. (❏ Read
Acts 8:5-17.) Philip was able to begin with a single verse in
the book of Isaiah and thoroughly explain who Jesus was
to an Ethiopian royal official. (❏ Read Acts 8:35.) Paul,
Priscilla and Aquila, and Apollos were all able to prove
that Jesus of Nazareth was the Messiah and Son of God,
using the Word of God as evidence. (❏ Read Acts 17:2-3;
11-12; 18:24-28.) Mature believers in the early church were
expected to know foundational teachings from the Word of
God and be able to apply and teach what they had studied.
(❏ Read 1 Timothy 3:1; 4:6-13; Titus 1:9; Hebrews 6:1-3.)
Jesus' followers saw studying and applying the Scriptures
as the only sure way to direct people to King Jesus and
to advance the purposes and power of His kingdom.

STUDYING AND APPLYING IN OUR LIVES

Paul instructed His son in the faith, Timothy, to diligently
study God's Word and faithfully apply that Word as
a fruitful worker. (❏ Read 2 Timothy 2:15.) Paul's
command to Timothy rings true for every one of us as
true disciples of Jesus. The term *rightly dividing* means
to cut in a straight line. It's like a skilled carpenter who
can make perfectly straight cuts in timber in order to
build something people need and can have confidence
in. Disciples of the Living Word of God are called to
rightly divide the Word of God in order to bless and
build up others. As followers of Jesus, we are called to

work in the Word in order to see the truth of the Word worked out in our lives and in the lives of others.

As students of God's Word, it is important that we understand that we are not to study and apply by our own strength or with our own wisdom. Rather, we are called to trust in the empowerment and guidance of the Holy Spirit. It is the Spirit of God who inspired the writing of the Word of God. (❏ Read 2 Timothy 3:16-17.) And, it is the Spirit of God who will teach us all things and lead us into all truth. (❏ Read John 14:26; 16:13.) He will help us know what the Word of God says, what it means, what it requires, and what it accomplishes. The Holy Spirit's light and life in studying and applying will ensure that the truth of God's Word will transform lives as He intends.

> *Disciples of the Living Word of God are called to rightly divide the Word of God in order to bless and build up others.*

MEMORIZE: *"Be diligent to present yourself approved to God, a worker who does not need to be ashamed, rightly dividing the word of truth."* (2 Timothy 2:15)

Use the following lines to write out the scripture to help you commit it to memory.

_____

_____

_____

_____

_____

_____

_____

KEY TRUTH: Disciples of Jesus follow His example of diligently studying and thoroughly applying the Word of God.

YOUR RESPONSE:

This is how you can respond in loving obedience to Jesus as you apply the truths from this lesson to your life.

- Ask Jesus to fill you with His Holy Spirit as you commit to be a life-long learner and doer of the Word of God.

- Use a daily reading guide to study through the entire Bible every year.

- Acknowledge the Holy Spirit every time you study the Word and ask Him to teach you all things and lead you into all truth.

- Find people who are mature in studying and applying God's Word. Ask them questions. Imitate and emulate their practices. Adopt their study tools. Be accountable to them for your study and application of God's Word.

WRITTEN RESPONSE: LESSON REVIEW

Review each section from the lesson on the previous pages to fill in each blank below. This review will help to reinforce the truths from this lesson in your life.

1. In the Scriptures, _____ means thoroughly _____ and _____ into something with the _____ of _____ it's true _____ and _____.

2. In the Scriptures, _____ means putting into _____ what is _____ and _____.

3. Through all of Jesus' _____ and _____, there came the _____ and _____ of all that God had _____ and all that God had _____.

4. Jesus' _____ saw _____ and _____ the Scriptures as the only sure way to _____ people to King Jesus and to _____ the _____ and _____ of His kingdom.

5. The Holy Spirit's _____ and _____ in _____ and _____ will ensure that the _____ of God's Word will _____ lives as He intends.

WRITTEN RESPONSE: LIFE REFLECTION

Using the journaling section on the pages at the end of this lesson,
write in your own words your responses to the following questions.

1. What have you learned and what has impacted you personally
    from this lesson?

2. In reading the scripture references in this lesson, what are you
    sensing and seeing the Holy Spirit highlighting and revealing to
    you that will enable you to better follow Jesus?

3. As a disciple and follower of Jesus, what steps of loving
    obedience do you need to take to see what you have learned in
    this lesson become ongoing practices and patterns in your life?

Journal

Journal

Lesson 5

———

FOLLOWING JESUS IN PRAYING AND PRAISING

Notes

PRAYING AND PRAISING INTRODUCTION
❏ *Read Luke 11:1-13 and 1 Peter 2:9-10*

Jesus, the One who spoke the universe into existence and holds it together by the word of His power, used His earthly voice for prevailing prayer and powerful praise. (❏ Read Hebrews 1:1-3.) Jesus lived a life of prayer marked by signs, wonders and miracles as He went. (❏ Read Luke 5:15-16.) Praying wasn't an occasional activity for Jesus, but rather a constant flow in His ministry to God and man. Jesus was also a Man of great praise. He displayed a life of profound gratitude to the Father, always rightly representing God's glory to others. In so doing, He accurately expressed who God was and what He had done, leaving an example for all God-honoring people to follow.

Every disciple of Jesus has joined a holy and royal priesthood and has been given a ministry of prayer and praise. (❏ Read 1 Peter 2:9-10.) It is the honor and inheritance of every disciple to live a life of answered prayer. It is the joy and privilege of every disciple to behold the greatness of the Father and the Son and boldly declare God's praises. Praying and praising like Jesus are top priorities and tremendous privileges for true disciples.

> *Praying and praising like Jesus are top priorities and tremendous privileges for true disciples.*

PRAYING AND PRAISING DEFINED

The words for *prayer* in the Bible have to do with making vocal, constant, faith-filled requests to God that are in accordance with His will for the earth. In the New Testament, prayer is an attitude as well as an action. It is an always-listening, ever-ready attitude to agree with the revealed will of God. The Apostle Paul instructed the Thessalonian church to pray without ceasing. (❏ Read 1 Thessalonians 5:17.) This doesn't mean a nonstop, uninterrupted flow of words and requests, but rather an attitude of ever-ready praying. Prayer is a disciple's ministry of an unending willingness and divine eagerness to pray to God at any time for anything the Holy Spirit directs us to pray. Prayer produces a powerful partnership between us and God. It isn't an attempt to overcome God's unwillingness to act on our behalf, but an exercise of accessing God's overwhelming willingness to act on our behalf, bringing man to God and God to man. (❏ Read Matthew 7:7-11.) Prayer is a lifestyle pattern of listening to the Spirit, receiving revelation concerning God's will, agreeing with God's will through faith-filled requests, and engaging God's provision and direction.

The words for *praise* in the Bible have to do with vocal declarations of the essence and exploits of God. God's essence is about who He is. God's exploits are about what He's done, is doing, and will do. Praise can be spoken, sung, accompanied by instruments or the lifting of hands.

Praise can provoke to action or pacify the soul to peace. Praise is full of faith, and accompanied by gratitude and rejoicing. Praise is an attitude of gratitude that becomes a vocal expression concerning God's goodness. The two primary books in the Bible that teach us about praise and worship are the book of Psalms and the book of Revelation. These books tell us that praise is about continually putting all of our focus on the Father and the Son. Praise is unceasing and triumphant. (❏ Read Psalm 34:1; Psalm 47:1; Revelation 4:8; Revelation 11:16-18.) God's praises should be great because He is great. (❏ Read Psalm 145:3; Revelation 5:13-14.)

PRAYING AND PRAISING IN THE LIFE OF JESUS

Jesus lived a life of constant prayer. In the first chapter of Mark we see Jesus in a solitary place praying to the Father, early in the morning, after a long evening of supernatural ministry. (❏ Read Mark 1:32-35.) In the third chapter of Luke we read about Jesus coming up from the waters of John's baptism praying and receiving the Holy Spirit. (❏ Read Luke 3:21-22.) The more Jesus' ministry progressed, and the more the crowds grew, the more Jesus withdrew to pray. (❏ Read Luke 5:16.) Whenever Jesus prayed, His petitions were actually answered. The constant in Christ's life of answered prayer was that He only did what He saw the Father doing and only said (including in prayer) what He heard the Father saying.

(❏ Read John 5:19; 12:49-50.) Jesus was always listening, receiving, agreeing, and engaging. He never had a doubt the Father was listening or that His petitions would be granted, because His life of prayer was aligned with the Father's will. (❏ Read John 11:41-42.)

Whenever Jesus prayed, His petitions were actually answered.

Jesus was a Man of great praise. Jesus was always revealing and lifting up the grace and goodness of the Father. For Jesus, praise was a proactive, faith-filled exercise that demonstrated to people His settled confidence in God's plan and provision. (❏ Read Matthew 14:19; 26:26; John 11:41.) In the gospel of Mark, we see that Jesus sang the Passover hymns with His disciples before heading to the cross. (❏ Read Mark 14:26.) This collection of hymns came from Psalms 115-118 and includes some of most profound praise language in the Bible. You couldn't be around Jesus without constantly hearing about the wonder and works of the Father.

PRAYING AND PRAISING IN THE LIVES OF JESUS' FOLLOWERS

The early church was steadfastly devoted to prayer. (❏ Read Acts 2:42; 6:4.) Guided by the Spirit, Christ's early followers lived lives of answered prayer. Salvation, healing, deliverance, miracles, provision, wisdom, and

Notes

divine protection were the norm for the early church. The reason for this was that the Father's will was discovered by the Spirit, and agreed with and accessed through faith-filled prayer. The apostle James declared that the prayer of faith had the power to profoundly impact human need at every level. (❑ Read James 5:13-18.) The apostle Paul exhorted the believers in Philippi to not worry about anything but pray about everything, believing that righteous requests would be met and rewarded. (❑ Read Philippians 4:6-7.)

From the moment Christ's disciples received the baptism with the Holy Spirit, the wonderful works of God were proclaimed. (❑ Read Acts 2:11.) The New Testament writers fill their letters with lavish praise to the Father and the Son. Any time the crowds wanted to ascribe praise to the apostles for mighty miracles, the apostles were quick to give glory to God. (❑ Read Acts 3:12-16; 14:8-18.) We see in the life of the apostle Paul that rejoicing in God's wonder and works was a constant in his life. (❑ Read Philippians 4:4; 1 Thessalonians 5:16.) He commanded the early churches not only to rejoice in everything, but to give thanks all the time for every single blessing of God. (❑ Read Ephesians 5:20; Philippians 4:6; 1 Thessalonians 5:18). The early church filled the

> *The early church filled the earth with God's good news and God's great praise.*

earth with God's good news and God's great praise.

PRAYING AND PRAISING IN OUR LIVES

If someone is going to follow Jesus, a life of prayer may be voluntary, but it is not optional. Jesus instructs us in His Word, "*when* you pray," not "*if* you pray." (❑ Read Matthew 6:6-15.) The key to a life of answered prayer is discovering the will of God and agreeing with it in faith. (❑ Read 1 John 5:14-15.) One of our challenges in prayer is that we don't know what to pray for as we ought to. (❑ Read Romans 8:26-27.) The answer in meeting this challenge is that God freely reveals His will to us through His Word and by His Spirit. Then, He calls us to lift our voices and confidently lay hold of His will being done. Directed by God's Spirit and anchored in God's Word, we are able to see the things God desires to do. When we ask in faith – free from doubt – for God's will to be done in the earth, we can be filled with confidence that our petitions will be granted. (❑ Read James 1:6-7.)

In the same way our praying must be led by the Spirit, our praising must be led by the Spirit as well. (❑ Read Ephesians 5:18-20; 1 Corinthians 14:15.) It was the Holy Spirit who inspired the writers of the Psalms to honor God for who He truly was. And it was the same Holy Spirit who revealed to the apostle John the Lord Jesus Christ in all of His splendor and glory. Likewise, the Holy Spirit will lead us as followers and disciples of Jesus who praise and

Notes

worship God in Spirit and in truth. (❑ Read John 4:21-24.) As disciples, we are called to fill the earth with the knowledge of the glory of our God. (❑ Read Habakkuk 2:14.) A

> *If someone is going to follow Jesus, a life of prayer may be voluntary, but it is not optional.*

primary way to accomplish this is through our ministry of perpetually praising the wonder and works of God.

As members of the royal priesthood under Jesus the High Priest, we are now priests of prayer and praise. The most important key to this ministry of prayer and praise is being led and empowered by the Holy Spirit. He reveals God's will in prayer. He gives us fresh revelation of the glory of the Father and the Son and the appropriate praise response. As disciples called to engage in a life of dynamic prayer and praise, we must follow Christ's example and the example of all who raised their voices to God and released His power in the earth.

MEMORIZE: *"Rejoice always, pray without ceasing, in everything give thanks; for this is the will of God in Christ Jesus for you."* (1 Thessalonians 5:16-18)

Use the following lines to write out the scripture to help you commit it to memory.

_____

_____

_____

_____

_____

_____

_____

KEY TRUTH: As disciples called to engage in a life of dynamic prayer and praise, we must follow Christ's example and the example of all who raised their voices to God and released His power in the earth.

YOUR RESPONSE:

This is how you can respond in loving obedience to Jesus as you apply the truths from this lesson to your life.

- Allow the Holy Spirit to empower you for an always-listening, ever-ready attitude of praying.

- As the Spirit reveals to you God's Word and God's will, agree with it in faith-filled prayer.

- Allow the Holy Spirit to reveal to you new revelations of the Father and the Son. Respond with words of faith-filled praise.

- Take every opportunity possible to rejoice in the Lord Jesus and to give God the Father thanks for all His blessings.

WRITTEN RESPONSE: LESSON REVIEW

Review each section from the lesson on the previous pages to fill in each blank below. This review will help to reinforce the truths from this lesson in your life.

1. Prayer is a _____ pattern of _____ to the Spirit, _____ _____ concerning God's will, _____ with God's will through _____ requests, and _____ God's _____ and _____.

2. The words for _____ in the Bible have to do with _____ _____ of the _____ and _____ of God.

3. The constant in Christ's _____ of _____ _____ was that He only _____ what He _____ the Father _____ and only _____ (including in _____) what He _____ the Father _____.

4. The early church _____ the earth with God's _____ _____ and God's _____ _____.

5. As _____ called to _____ in a life of dynamic _____ and _____, we must follow _____ example and the example of _____ who _____ their _____ to God and _____ His _____ in the earth.

WRITTEN RESPONSE: LIFE REFLECTION

Using the journaling section on the pages at the end of this lesson, write in your own words your responses to the following questions.

1. What have you learned and what has impacted you personally from this lesson?

2. In reading the scripture references in this lesson, what are you sensing and seeing the Holy Spirit highlighting and revealing to you that will enable you to better follow Jesus?

3. As a disciple and follower of Jesus, what steps of loving obedience do you need to take to see what you have learned in this lesson become ongoing practices and patterns in your life?

Journal

Journal

Journal

Lesson 6

FOLLOWING JESUS IN CONFESSING AND FORGIVING

CONFESSING AND FORGIVING
INTRODUCTION

❏ *Read Luke 11:1-4; Matthew 6:5-14*

Jesus' disciples saw first-hand how His life of prayer to the Father produced dynamic, life-changing results. They wanted to know what He knew about prayer, do what He did in prayer and receive the results He received in prayer. So, one day, after Jesus had finished a season of prayer, one of His disciples asked Him to teach them how to pray as their Master and Lord. He responded to their request with dynamic *words* of prayer that revealed a dynamic *way* of praying. Contained in this prayer we find these words: "*And forgive us our sins, for we also forgive everyone who is indebted to us.*"

On a previous occasion, Jesus had given His followers principles of prayer, practices of prayer and a pattern for prayer that would help them rightly relate to God, to one another and to the world. He said this pattern for praying would release God's kingdom power and glory to establish His divine purposes in the earth. In this teaching on prayer we find these words: "*And forgive us our debts, as we forgive our debtors.*" And, "*For if you forgive men their trespasses, your heavenly Father will also forgive you. But if you do not forgive men their trespasses, neither will your Father forgive your trespasses.*"

In both instances, Jesus emphasized the need for confessing one's sins against God and others and forgiving another's sins against them to remain clear and clean before God and others. Jesus taught that everything in His kingdom worked on the basis of being right with God, right with oneself and right with others. Jesus taught that right relationships would release His righteous rule. Confessing and forgiving are at the very heart of this. Jesus taught that agreeing with God about the nature of what sin is and naming it (confessing) is vital to relational integrity with the Father. And He taught that acknowledging the sinful debt of others and canceling it (forgiving) was vital to relational integrity as well.

> *Jesus taught that everything in His kingdom worked on the basis of being right with God, right with oneself and right with others.*

CONFESSING AND FORGIVING DEFINED

In the Scriptures, the words *confess, confession* or *confessing* have to do with honestly and truthfully acknowledging and agreeing with God concerning sin and righteousness. Confessing then can have to do with acknowledging and agreeing with God concerning sound doctrine or sinful deeds. We are to hang on to everything that is faithful and true, and to let go of everything that is false, unworthy and unclean. It is important that we understand that sin comes out of the life from a repentant heart by way of the mouth. Confessing sin isn't so much about saying "I'm sorry" as saying "I did it." Confessing sin is saying the same thing about sin as God says. We are called to be a people who continuously confess sin to God and to others we have in any way violated or wronged.

> *... sin comes out of the life from a repentant heart by way of the mouth.*

In the Scriptures, the words *forgive, forgiveness* or *forgiving* have to do with the canceling of a moral or spiritual debt on the basis of a price being paid by another. God forgives and cancels the debts of sinful mankind through the sacrifice of His Son, Jesus. In the Old Testament, the blood of animals temporarily appeased the demands of a righteous and holy God. In the New Testament, the blood of the Lamb of God, Jesus Christ, fully and eternally redeems and reconciles man to God and to one another. When we confess our sins to God, we are forgiven on the basis of the price for sin having already been paid by Jesus. When we confess our sins to one another, we forgive one another on the exact same basis. As God has forgiven or canceled our debt in Christ Jesus, so we forgive or cancel one another's debts in Christ Jesus.

CONFESSING AND FORGIVING IN THE LIFE OF JESUS

John the Baptist came preaching a message of repenting and believing in the coming Messiah through confessing sins and consecrating one's self to receive His mission, message and ministry. (❏ Read Matthew 3:1-12.) On the heels of John's declaration of how to prepare for the coming of the King and His kingdom, Jesus came with the same call and command. (❏ Read Mark 1:14-15.) Jesus came from heaven to earth to bring the fullness of God's grace and truth, helping people to be honest with God about who they were, who His Christ was and how to find their way back to Him. (❏ Read John 1:14-16.) In the Sermon on the Mount, Jesus confronted the need for people to look first to the sin in their own lives and honestly acknowledge it before examining sin in someone else's life. (❏ Read Matthew 7:1-5.) Jesus came to reveal sin and righteousness, darkness and light, death and life. He

Jesus came to reveal sin and righteousness, darkness and light, death and life.

called men to confess sin and to confess Him as the way of truth and life that reconciled relationships with God, with self and with others. (❏ Read Matthew 10:32; John 14:1-6.)

In all of Jesus' dealings with people while on earth, he embodied a message of forgiving others on the basis of God's grace through the offering of His Sinless Son. (❏ Read John 3:14-17.) He called people to receive the loving offer of a forgiving Father and then to release that same love in forgiving others. (❏ Read Luke 17:3.) Near the end of His earthly ministry, He gave His disciples a command to love one another in the same measure and by the same means He had loved them—the love of God the Father in and through Him. (❏ Read John 13:31-35.) This love included completely forgiving one another, unmistakably marking them out as His followers and disciples. At the Last Supper, Jesus' final celebration of the Passover with His disciples, Jesus said that His blood would provide the payment for the forgiveness of sins that the Father desired to release. (❏ Read Matthew 26:27-28.)

CONFESSING AND FORGIVING IN THE LIVES OF JESUS' FOLLOWERS

In the writings of Christ's disciples, the message of confessing and forgiving is clear. The Apostle John wrote that coming into agreement with God's assessment of sin and honestly acknowledging it would result in forgiveness and cleansing from unrighteousness. (❏ Read 1 John 1:8-9.) It is important to note that the forgiveness and cleansing John is referring to with God is *relational* and not *salvational*. Having been reconciled to God through repentance and faith in Christ, the confession of sin is now about restored relational intimacy with Him. The Apostle James wrote that confessing our sins one to another and praying for one another in faith removes a relational impediment and opens a divine door to all manner of healing and health. (❏ Read James 5:16.) In the New Testament, it is clear that three main obstacles to receiving answers to prayer are unbelief, unconfessed sin and unforgiveness. Jesus' followers taught that these obstacles must be confronted and conquered if one is to live in the free flow of God's love and power.

> In the New Testament, it is clear that three main obstacles to receiving answers to prayer are unbelief, unconfessed sin and unforgiveness.

Time and again the Apostle Paul emphasized the need for followers of Jesus to forgive one another in the same manner they had been forgiven in Christ. (❏ Read Ephesians 4:31-32; Colossians 3:12-13.) The standard of forgiving others that they were to live by was the standard that had been established by God the Father through the redemptive work of Jesus the Son—forgiving people's debt of sin completely. Even an early church leader named Stephen who had been assaulted and killed by a mob resistant to his message, forgave his attackers and asked God to do the same. (❏ Read Acts 7:59-60.) He basically

Notes repeated the same words his Lord had spoken concerning His tormentors while on the cross. (❑ Read Luke 23:34.) In the Scriptures and throughout church history the response of true believers and followers of Jesus who have been sinned against has always been the same— forgiving those sins according to the limitless forgiveness extended by a loving Father through His Saving Son.

CONFESSING AND FORGIVING IN OUR LIVES

So, the standard and strategy for confessing and forgiving in our lives is clear—fully agree with God and acknowledge sin in our own lives while we fully forgive the ways in which others have sinned against us. We first confront and confess sins we have committed, enabling us then to accurately and appropriately forgive others their debt of sin toward us. This is what will keep us righteously relating to God and others. A lack of consistency in this area will compromise the integrity and intimacy of our relationships with God the Father and Jesus the Son, diminishing the voice of the Holy Spirit in our lives. (❑ Read Ephesians 4:25-30.) It will also compromise the integrity and intimacy of our relationships with others.

Being honest to God and loving to all is foundational in being a true disciple and follower of Jesus.

Being honest to God and loving to all is foundational in being a true disciple and follower of Jesus. Being honest and humble in an age of dishonesty and pride enables us to be counter culture Christians who live by the kingdom values of grace and truth. (❑ Read John 1:16-17.) Being loving to all resists the human tendency to repay evil for evil and reveals the Lord's heart of overcoming evil with good. (❑ Read Luke 23:34; Romans 12:17-21.) As faithful followers of Jesus, confessing and forgiving are to become a lifestyle that leads to reconciled relationships with God and man.

MEMORIZE: *"And forgive us our debts, as we forgive our debtors."* (Matthew 6:12)

Use the following lines to write out the scripture to help you commit it to memory.

_____

_____

_____

_____

_____

_____

_____

KEY TRUTH: Jesus emphasized the need for confessing one's sins against God and others and forgiving another's sins against them to remain clear and clean before God and others.

YOUR RESPONSE:

This is how you can respond in loving obedience to Jesus as you apply the truths from this lesson to your life.

- Ask the Holy Spirit to reveal sinful attitudes and actions in your life, confessing them one by one to God in humility and honesty.

- Ask the Holy Spirit to reveal instances where you need to forgive others who have sinned against you, forgiving them from the heart as you cancel their debt and release them to Christ.

- Make a fresh and new commitment to first look at and confront sin in your own life before looking at sin in the lives of others, and daily take your debts to the Lord in confession and cleansing while you release others from their debts in faith and forgiveness.

- Find someone younger than you, either spiritually or chronologically, that you can humbly and honestly share these principles with.

WRITTEN RESPONSE: LESSON REVIEW

Review each section from the lesson on the previous pages to fill in each blank below. This review will help to reinforce the truths from this lesson in your life.

1. _____ sin is _____ the
   _____ thing about sin as _____
   says. We are called to be a people who _____
   _____ sin to God and to others we have in
   any way _____ or _____.

2. As God has _____ or _____ our debt
   in Christ Jesus, so we _____ or _____
   one another's _____ in Christ Jesus.

3. He called men to _____ sin and to
   _____ Him as the way of truth and life that
   _____ relationships with _____,
   with _____ and with _____.

4. In the New Testament, it is clear that three main
   _____ to receiving _____
   to prayer are _____, _____
   _____ and _____.

5. So, the _____ and _____ for
   _____ and _____ in our lives is clear—
   fully _____ with God and _____
   sin in our own lives while we fully _____
   the ways in which others have sinned against us.

WRITTEN RESPONSE: LIFE REFLECTION

Using the journaling section on the pages at the end of this lesson, write in your own words your responses to the following questions.

1. What have your learned and what has impacted you personally from this lesson?

2. In reading the scripture references in this lesson, what are you sensing and seeing the Holy Spirit highlighting and revealing to you that will enable you to better follow Jesus?

3. As a disciple and follower of Jesus, what steps of loving obedience do you need to take to see what you have learned in this lesson become ongoing practices and patterns in your life?

Journal

Journal

FOLLOWING JESUS IN WORSHIPING AND WORKING

WORSHIPING AND WORKING INTRODUCTION

❏ *Read Romans 12:1-2*

Everything a disciple says and does is to be an offering of worship to God. No one modeled this better than Jesus Christ. His every word and work were an offering of wholehearted worship to the Father. Through Moses, God gave the Law (the first five books of the Bible), to show people what was righteous and to provide a way for people to worship and to commune with God through various sacrifices. (❏ Read Deuteronomy 10:12-15.) Through the writers of the Psalms and the Prophets, worship was shown to be an ongoing offering of love and devotion to God. (❏ Read 1 Samuel 15:22; Psalm 40:6-7; Hosea 6:6.) Through Jesus, all righteousness was fulfilled as He became the perfect sacrifice to open the way to intimate spiritual and daily worship to the Father. In Christ Jesus worship was revealed as one's life laid down in sacrifice and surrender to a worthy and trustworthy God.

Worshiping and working was the primary purpose for which the Savior rose each morning. Christ's work on earth was always an act of worship through a surrendered heart and life unto God. Every word spoken from His mouth and deed done with His hands was an offering of excellence and extravagance unto God. No one could mistake the One whom Jesus lived to worship. And, as followers of Jesus, no one should mistake the One whom we worship as

Worshiping and working was the primary purpose for which the Savior rose each morning.

well. A disciple of Jesus follows His example of making every attitude of the heart, thought of the mind, word of the mouth, and deed with the hands an offering of worship to the Father. In this, worshiping and working become a holy habit of making everything said and done a suitable sacrifice unto God.

WORSHIPING AND WORKING DEFINED

The primary word for *worship* in the New Testament has to do with kneeling or lying face-down to show respect and honor for someone. It also has to do with showing deep affection and allegiance to the authority of another. It is making oneself low to make someone else high. It is the laying down of one for the lifting up of another. Throughout history, people viewed worship as a specific action at a particular time in a distinct place. When Jesus came, He clarified the intent, content and extent of worship. He said that the intent was

The primary word for worship in the New Testament has to do with kneeling or lying face-down to show respect and honor for someone.

Notes

Notes

to honor God for who He truly was. He said that the content was to be spiritually vital, genuine and authentic. And, He said that the extent was to be about everyone and everything at all times. (❑ Read John 4:21-24.)

WORSHIPING AND WORKING IN THE LIFE OF JESUS

According to the writer of Hebrews, Jesus fulfilled King David's words that what God ultimately desired was a willing life laid down as a worthy sacrifice. (❑ Read Psalm 40:6-8; Hebrews 10:5-10.) Nothing Jesus said or did was merely an outward religious ritual, but rather an inward dedication and devotion. The words of His mouth and the meditation of His heart were always well-pleasing to the Father. (❑ Read Psalm 19:14.) When Jesus came up from the waters of baptism, and was later transfigured on the mountain, God the Father thundered words of love and pleasure for and in the Son. (❑ Read Matthew 3:17;

Jesus lived a life of well-pleasing worship and work to the Father.

17:5.) Jesus lived a life of well-pleasing worship and work to the Father. When Paul called on the Ephesians to be imitators of God, he appealed to the ultimate example of worshiping and working in the life of the Son. (❑ Read Ephesians 5:1-2.) From beginning to end, and everywhere in between, Jesus' words and work were worship. Jesus was diligent in seeing His work as worship. Daily,

Christ entered into the work of His Father. (❏ Read John 5:17-19.) The Lord went so far as to say that His necessary food and fulfillment were to finish the work given Him by the Father. (❏ Read John 4:34.) As was stated before, there was no mistaking the One for whom Jesus lived. The honor and true worship of the Father was Christ's highest priority. His steps of worship-working became His passionate pathway that all true disciples should follow.

WORSHIPING AND WORKING IN THE LIVES OF JESUS' FOLLOWERS

The early disciples of Jesus would not tolerate any worship that was false or work that was of the flesh. The worship of anything or anyone other than the Father and the Son was forbidden. Trying to do the works of God other than by the power of the Holy Spirit was also forbidden. Holding all things in common, prayer, doctrine, preaching the Gospel, signs and wonders, care for widows, and stewardship of resources were all forms of worship-working for the early church. (❏ Read Acts 2:42-47; 3:19-20; 4:32-37; 6:1-7.)

The Apostle Paul taught the churches to lead lives of worshiping and working. (❏ Read 2 Corinthians 6:16-7:1.) The writer of Hebrews helped his audience understand that worship was no longer about the rituals of the Law but the lifestyle of Christ. (❏ Read Hebrews 2:10-3:1; 7:20-28.) The Apostle Peter explained that believers are a holy priesthood – a spiritual temple

99

Notes

of living stones – who offer up acceptable worship to the Father and the Son. (❏ Read 1 Peter 2:4-5.)

WORSHIPING AND WORKING IN OUR LIVES

Today, it can be easy to believe that worship is solely about singing songs when the saints are gathered. Singing with the people of God is certainly an expression of worship. But singing is just one expression of worship, not the only expression of worship. Worship is about the attitudes of our hearts, the thoughts of our minds, the words of our mouths, and the deeds of our hands. Prayer is worship. Studying the Word of God is worship. Preaching the Gospel is worship. Serving our families is worship. Our occupational work is worship. Serving our local church is worship. Stewarding the resources God entrusts to us is worship. Worship is about being wholly devoted and dedicated to God the Father and Jesus the Son through the indwelling work of the Holy Spirit.

> *Worship is about the attitudes of our hearts, the thoughts of our minds, the words of our mouths, and the deeds of our hands.*

The Scriptures refer to us as the temple of the Holy Spirit. (❏ Read 1 Corinthians 3:16; 2 Corinthians 6:16-18.) As the temple of the Holy Spirit, disciples and followers of Jesus now become walking, talking, working worshipers. Even our work for those in authority over us should be considered worship to the Lord. (❏ Read Colossians 3:23-24.) As we have seen, Jesus lived a life of wholehearted, fully integrated worshiping and working, and we must do the same.

MEMORIZE: *"I beseech you therefore, brethren, by the mercies of God, that you present your bodies a living sacrifice, holy, acceptable to God, which is your reasonable service."* (Romans 12:1)

Use the following lines to write out the scripture to help you commit it to memory.

_____

_____

_____

_____

_____

_____

_____

KEY TRUTH: Worship is about the attitudes of our hearts, the thoughts of our minds, the words of our mouths, and the deeds of our hands.

YOUR RESPONSE:

This is how you can respond in loving obedience to Jesus as you apply the truths from this lesson to your life.

- Take time each day in the secret place to freshly present your life as an offering of worship to God.

- Ask the Holy Spirit to identify any attitudes, thoughts, words, or deeds that do not bring the Father and the Son pure worship. Repent and remove these things. Commit to a life of worshiping and working.

- Prayerfully commit every situation of your day to worshiping the Father and the Son.

- Ask the Holy Spirit to empower you to worship God with excellence in every area of life.

WRITTEN RESPONSE: LESSON REVIEW

Review each section from the lesson on the previous pages to fill in each blank below. This review will help to reinforce the truths from this lesson in your life.

1. _____ and _____ was the _____ purpose for which the _____ rose _____ morning.

2. The primary word for _____ in the New Testament has to do with _____ or _____ _____ to show _____ and _____ for someone.

3. The honor and true _____ of the Father was Christ's _____ priority. His steps of _____- _____ became His passionate _____ that all true _____ should _____.

4. The Apostle Peter explained that _____ are a holy _____ – a spiritual _____ of living _____ – who offer up acceptable _____ to the Father and the Son.

5. Worship is about the attitudes of our _____, the thoughts of our _____, the words of our _____, and the deeds of our _____.

WRITTEN RESPONSE: LIFE REFLECTION

Using the journaling section on the pages at the end of this lesson, write in your own words your responses to the following questions.

1. What have your learned and what has impacted you personally from this lesson?

2. In reading the scripture references in this lesson, what are you sensing and seeing the Holy Spirit highlighting and revealing to you that will enable you to better follow Jesus?

3. As a disciple and follower of Jesus, what steps of loving obedience do you need to take to see what you have learned in this lesson become ongoing practices and patterns in your life?

Journal

Journal

—

FOLLOWING JESUS IN EVANGELIZING AND DISCIPLING

EVANGELIZING AND DISCIPLING INTRODUCTION

☐ *Read Matthew 28:18-20; Mark 16:15-18; Luke 24:46-49*

Right before Jesus ascended into heaven after His crucifixion and resurrection, He gave His disciples what is called the Great Commission, or Supreme Commission. He told them that they were to go into the whole world, preaching the gospel to each and every person, making passionate, proficient and powerful followers of all who repented and believed in and on Him. In other words, He was calling and commissioning them to evangelize and disciple the people of the earth as their primary purpose and ultimate destiny. Souls saved and disciples made was to be their mission, message and ministry—their main reason for living.

Jesus' final words were that His disciples and followers should go everywhere evangelizing and discipling. His final words were to be their first works. They believed Him and committed themselves to do that very thing, and so should we. Evangelizing and discipling are to be our main reasons for rising each day to meet a world lost and broken, in need of being reached with the love

All other things in our lives, however important they may be, must be secondary to our primary calling to save souls and make disciples.

110

and power of God in Christ Jesus. All other things in our
lives, however important they may be, must be secondary
to our primary calling to save souls and make disciples.

EVANGELIZING AND DISCIPLING DEFINED

Evangelizing is declaring, defining, defending and
demonstrating God's gospel (good news) of salvation
through the life, death, resurrection and ascension of Jesus
Christ, the Son of God. *Declaring* the gospel has to do with
what it says. *Defining* the gospel has to do with what it
means. *Defending* the gospel has to do with why it's true.
Demonstrating the gospel has to do with what it does.
Evangelizing is clearly communicating the message of
God's plan to redeem, reconcile and restore sinful mankind
through His sinless Son, and compellingly confirming
this message with the signs of love and power that follow.
(❑ Read Mark 16:19-20; Acts 1:1-3, 8; 10:36-43.)

The following is a very helpful definition of
the gospel from Evangelist Rice Broocks:

> *The gospel is the good news that God became
> man in Jesus Christ. He lived the life we should
> have lived and died the death we should have
> died—in our place. Three days later, He rose
> from the dead, proving He is the Son of God and
> offering the gift of salvation and forgiveness of
> sins to anyone who repents and believes in Him.*

Notes

This is the message that sets men free from the penalty, power, guilt and shame of sin when it is acted upon through repenting and believing. (❏ Read John 3:14-17.)

Discipling is the process of taking believers from spiritual infancy to maturity as they are taught to love and obey Jesus in everything He has commanded, and as they are trained to be faithful and fruitful followers of Jesus in word and deed. On one hand, making and shaping new believers into highly functional disciples can happen in a relatively short span of time. (❏ Read Acts 6:1-7.) On another hand, we become more and more mature and devoted and dynamic disciples over the course of our lifetime. (❏ Read 2 Timothy 2:1-2; 2 Peter 3:17-18.) We are to help believers lay a good foundation of faith and faithfulness, strong and stable enough on which to build a life in Jesus. (❏ Read Matthew 7:24-27.) Then, we are to ongoingly develop believers as they continue to grow in faith and endurance through time, teaching, testing, trial and triumph. (❏ Read James 1:2-4.)

EVANGELIZING AND DISCIPLING IN THE LIFE OF JESUS

Jesus' earthly ministry was given in large part to the declaration and demonstration of the gospel of the kingdom and to equipping disciples to give witness to what they had heard and seen in Him. (❏ Read Matthew 10:1-4; Mark 3:13-18; Luke 6:12-19.) He clearly communicated

God's plan of redemption through the offering of His Son—
the Messiah, Savior and King. He called men to respond to
His message and ministry and then to call others to do the
same. In a little over three years, Jesus made disciples and
trained apostles out of those He had called to follow Him
and learn of His Father's
Word, will and ways.

*Jesus' earthly ministry
was given in large part
to the declaration and
demonstration of the
gospel of the kingdom
and to equipping
disciples to give witness
to what they had heard
and seen in Him.*

While He was still on
earth, He sent them out
to preach the gospel and
to extend and express
God's grace to heal the
human experience—
spirit, soul and body.
(❑ Read Luke 9:1-6;
10:1-9.) He modeled for
His followers how to
heal the sick and cast out the demonic hordes that sought
to bind and torment. (❑ Read Matthew 12:22-30.) He left
a gospel witness in every village, town and city that He
went to as part of His plan to heal those oppressed of the
devil, and to raise up and release a generation of Spirit-
filled world changers who would carry on His mission
of saving and healing after He ascended to heaven.

EVANGELIZING AND DISCIPLING IN THE LIVES OF JESUS' FOLLOWERS

As we have stated, when Jesus was still on earth, His followers watched Him work, worked with Him and were sent out by Him to do the works of God to rescue and restore in His mighty name. Upon His departure, Jesus commissioned His followers to carry out His kingdom cause of seeking, serving and saving the lost, broken and bound and to bring spiritual formation into their lives, making them more and more the people of God the Father and Jesus the Son. From the outpouring of the Holy Spirit on the Day of Pentecost, they went about evangelizing and discipling.

(❏ Read Acts 2:1-42.) They preached good news, performed good works, and planted Spirit-filled, covenantal communities. (❏ Read Acts 14:21-28.) They equipped believers in Jesus to be people steadfastly devoted to the Word of God, and to engage in authentic spiritual fellowship

Jesus' apostles wrote extensively about evangelizing and discipling.

and friendship with one another. They lived life together in Jesus praying, praising, and seeking God individually and corporately. (❏ Read Acts 2:42.) They made disciples who understood that they were to represent Christ in the earth and to reflect His glory in everything they said and everything they did. (❏ Read Acts 6:1-7.)

Jesus' apostles wrote extensively about evangelizing and discipling. The Apostle Paul taught the believers at Ephesus that Jesus had made every provision to give gifts to men and make gifts of men. He taught them to thoroughly and dynamically equip His disciples and followers to grow and build His Church numerically and spiritually. (❑ Read Ephesians 4:7-16; 2 Timothy 2:2.) The Apostle Peter exhorted believers to winsomely and wisely declare, define, defend and demonstrate the gospel, convincing unbelievers and building their lives. (❑ Read 1 Peter 2:1-10; 3:15-16.)

EVANGELIZING AND DISCIPLING IN OUR LIVES

The message should be clear: *evangelizing* and *discipling* are our primary purposes and priorities. To see souls saved and disciples made is the main reason we rise every day. This is our great and supreme calling and commission with life-giving consequences now and throughout eternity. Getting the gospel to everyone, everywhere and making disciples of those who believe in and on Jesus is the greatest gift we can give to others and the greatest privilege we could possibly be granted. If we want to be filled with joy and a daily sense of fulfilling our divine destiny, we must give our lives for what Jesus and His followers gave theirs—share God's gift of eternal life and use it to shape generations of future followers who do the same.

Evangelist Rice Broocks trains people to use something called the *S.A.L.T. Principle* to share the gospel and shape people's beliefs in the Word, will and ways of God. The first step is to *Start a conversation*. When we engage people in a gospel conversation, we open the door to a divine dialogue that can produce dynamic results. The next steps are to *Ask questions* and *Listen*. Asking questions and listening communicates interest in someone's story, beliefs and perspective. A sincere interview can turn into a sincere invitation to consider the claims of Christ and the eternal purpose of God. Finally, *Tell the story*. First, tell *God's story*. That is the gospel of grace through the offering of the sinless Son, Jesus. Then, tell *your story*. That is how the gospel has impacted and influenced your life for eternal good. This is your testimony, or evidence for the case for Christ's power to save, heal and deliver. The *S.A.L.T. Principle* is a useful principle and process for both evangelizing and discipling.

> *To see souls saved and disciples made is the main reason we rise every day.*

MEMORIZE: *"And Jesus came and spoke to them, saying, 'All authority has been given to Me in heaven and earth. Go therefore and make disciples of all the nations, baptizing them in the name of the Father and of the Son and of the Holy Spirit, teaching them to observe all things that I have commanded you; and lo, I am with you always, even to the end of the age. Amen.'"* (Matthew 28:18-20)

Use the following lines to write out the scripture to help you commit it to memory.

_____

_____

_____

_____

_____

_____

_____

KEY TRUTH: Evangelizing and discipling are our primary purposes and priorities. To see souls saved and disciples made is the main reason we rise every day.

YOUR RESPONSE:

This is how you can respond in loving obedience to Jesus as you apply the truths from this lesson to your life.

- Make a fresh commitment each day to give yourself to your primary purpose of evangelizing and discipling.

- Ask the Holy Spirit to guide and empower you to lead people to faith in Christ and to help them to grow strong in Him. Use Evangelist Rice Broocks' definition of the gospel and the S.A.L.T. Principle to help to that end.

- The best way to guide people through the process of evangelizing and discipling is to use good written tools created by people gifted to equip believers for the work of evangelizing and discipling. Find proven resources that produce real results and use them regularly.

- The first tool, of course, is the Scriptures—the very Word and words of God. Read the Scriptures, meditate on them, memorize them and use them in evangelizing and discipling for the glory of God and the good of others.

WRITTEN RESPONSE: LESSON REVIEW

Review each section from the lesson on the previous pages to fill in each blank below. This review will help to reinforce the truths from this lesson in your life.

1. _____ is _____, _____, _____ and _____ God's gospel (good news) of salvation through the _____, _____, _____ and _____ of Jesus Christ, the Son of God.

2. _____ is the process of taking believers from spiritual _____ to _____ as they are taught to _____ and _____ Jesus in _____ He has commanded, and as they are trained to be _____ and _____ followers of Jesus in _____ and _____.

3. Jesus' earthly _____ was given in large part to the _____ and _____ of the gospel of the _____ and to _____ disciples to give _____ to what they had _____ and _____ in Him.

4. Upon His departure, Jesus _____ His followers to carry out His _____ cause of _____, _____ and _____ the lost, broken and bound and to bring _____ formation into their lives, making them _____ and _____

the people of God the Father and Jesus the Son.

5. The message should be clear: _____ and
_____ are our primary _____ and
_____. To see _____ saved and
_____ made is the main _____ we
_____ every day.

WRITTEN RESPONSE: LIFE REFLECTION

Using the journaling section on the pages at the end of this lesson,
write in your own words your responses to the following questions.

1. What have your learned and what has impacted you personally
   from this lesson?

2. In reading the scripture references in this lesson, what are you
   sensing and seeing the Holy Spirit highlighting and revealing to
   you that will enable you to better follow Jesus?

3. As a disciple and follower of Jesus, what steps of loving
   obedience do you need to take to see what you have learned in
   this lesson become ongoing practices and patterns in your life?

Journal

Journal

Journal

FOLLOWING JESUS IN RESISTING AND OVERCOMING

RESISTING AND OVERCOMING INTRODUCTION

❏ *Read Matthew 4:1-11*

The Eternal Son of God became a man. He was fully God and *fully* man. As such, He lived a life of divinity and humanity producing victory. He won every battle against the temptations that the world's culture threw at Him. He won every battle against the weaknesses of His human flesh. He won every battle against the schemes and resistance of the devil. How did He do it? First, He understood He was in a war with the world, the flesh, and the devil. Jesus is the Commander of Heaven's armies. (❏ Read Revelation 19:11-16.) Every day, Jesus rose up to join the fight. Second, He understood and embraced His limitations as a man. He put all His confidence in the will of His Heavenly Father and the work of the Holy Spirit. Christ's ability to walk in victory was found in His anointing with the Holy Spirit from God the Father. (❏ Read Acts 10:38.) Finally, Jesus used the truth of God's Word and the power of God's authority as His weapons.

Jesus' disciples followed His example. They learned how to conquer a love for the world by doing the will of their Heavenly Father. (❏ Read 1 John 2:15-17.) They learned how to conquer the lusts of their flesh by walking in the Spirit. (❏ Read Galatians 5:16.) They learned how to conquer the devil's schemes by resisting him in faith, exercising Christ's authority, and speaking the Word of

Resisting and overcoming is the call of every disciple.

God in Spirit-led prayer. (❏ Read Ephesians 6:10-18.) Resisting and overcoming is the call of every disciple. Christ Jesus, our Master, calls us to follow Him in resisting and overcoming unto total victory.

RESISTING AND OVERCOMING DEFINED

The Apostle James tells us that in our dealings with the enemy of our soul, the devil, we are to resist him steadfastly. (❏ Read James 4:7.) The word *resist* in this verse means to vigorously oppose, bravely resist, stand face-to-face against an adversary, and stand your ground. As believers, we are in a war. It's not a physical war, but a spiritual war. In this spiritual war, there are three main enemies we fight: the world, the flesh, and the devil. (❏ Read Ephesians 2:1-3.) The term *world* isn't a reference to the physical planet, but to the evil that is working in the world's systems and culture. The *flesh* refers to the law of sin and death in our physical bodies. The flesh can be tempted to sin, producing lusts (or desires) for things not of God. The *devil* refers to Satan, a fallen angel, and to the demons under his control and command.

When considering all the difficulties one might face in trying to live for God, the Apostle Paul assures us

that by God's love and
power complete victory
is ours. (❏ Read Romans
8:37.) In this verse, Paul
refers to us as *more than
conquerors*, which means
to be super overcomers who
overwhelmingly overpower
an enemy and achieve abundant victory. The Bible tells
us that we overcome the world through our faith in the
person and power of Jesus Christ. (❏ Read 1 John 5:4-5.)
Overcoming is possible through complete confidence in
Jesus. But, how do we know we have complete confidence
(faith and belief) in Jesus? By saying what He said
and doing what He did in resisting and overcoming.

> *In this spiritual war,
> there are three main
> enemies we fight:
> the world, the flesh,
> and the devil.*

RESISTING AND OVERCOMING IN THE LIFE OF JESUS

The three greatest episodes where we see Jesus resisting
and overcoming are His forty days in the wilderness
(❏ Read Luke 4:1-13), His prayers in the garden of
Gethsemane (❏ Read Matthew 26:36-46), and His
suffering and death on the cross (❏ Read Luke 23:39-49;
John 19:25-30). While in the wilderness, Jesus fasted forty
days enduring every temptation that Satan presented to
Him. He overcame the lust and pride of the world. He
defeated the demands of His flesh and resisted every work
of the devil by the power of the Holy Spirit. In the garden

of Gethsemane, as the Lord's betrayal and suffering drew near, He prayed to the Father. Jesus, feeling the onset of unprecedented suffering, asked the Father if there was any other way for mankind to be redeemed, reconciled and restored. Being assured there wasn't, Jesus overcame His flesh and the temptation to save Himself, as He put His confidence in the Father's will and the Spirit's work. While on the cross, Jesus resisted every temptation to ease or escape His sufferings. He overcame all pain and humiliation by His passion for the Father's will, His joy for salvation's work, and His trust in the Spirit's provision and power. (❏ Read Hebrews 12:2.)

Throughout Jesus' life, we see Him using the truth of God's Word as His primary weapon.

Throughout Jesus' life, we see Him using the truth of God's Word as His primary weapon. In the wilderness, every temptation was met with the bold declaration of God's Word. In Gethsemane, Jesus armed Himself with faith in God's will as revealed in God's Word. On the cross, Jesus quoted Scripture and fought His way through the torment and temptation with truth. After He rose from the dead, He revealed to His disciples that every battle fought and victory won – the resisting and overcoming – had already been laid out in God's Word. (❏ Read Luke 24:44-48.)

Notes

RESISTING AND OVERCOMING IN THE LIVES OF JESUS' FOLLOWERS

The Lord's disciples experienced first-hand what it was like to dominate demons by His authority. (❑ Read Luke 9:1-2.) Following the day of Pentecost, the early church used the authority of Jesus, the truth of God's Word, and faith in both to resist and overcome. Peter and John resisted and overcame the taunts and threats of the religious leaders by stating they would believe and obey God instead of the people who were denying and disobeying God. (❑ Read Acts 4:18-20.) Peter and John's companions resisted and overcame discouragement and fear with the truth of God's Word, faith in Christ's work, and the power of the Holy Spirit. (❑ Read Acts 4:23-33.) The early church resisted and overcame persecution from the world by declaring and demonstrating the truth of the Word everywhere they went. (❑ Read Acts 8:4-8.) The Apostle Peter resisted and overcame his prejudice and limited perspective concerning Gentiles by obeying the Holy Spirit and putting His faith in the commands he received from Jesus. (❑ Read Acts 10:9-48.) The Apostle Paul and his companions resisted and overcame the world's evil systems through preaching the Word of God, walking in the power of the Holy Spirit, and keeping their confidence in Jesus. (❑ Read Acts 14:21-22; 19:10-20.)

The Apostle Paul taught the churches that resisting and overcoming is the duty and privilege of all disciples. While the devil's schemes are many and powerful, the resources of the kingdom of God are greater in number and infinitely more powerful. (❏ Read Ephesians 6:10-18; 2 Corinthians 10:3-5.) Jesus' disciples believed Him when He said that He had given them authority over all the power of the enemy. (❏ Read Luke 10:18-20; Mark 16:15-20.)

RESISTING AND OVERCOMING IN OUR LIVES

The enemies the Lord and His followers faced – the world, the flesh, and the devil – are the same enemies all disciples face today. The enemies seeking our defeat haven't changed. The strategies for resisting and overcoming haven't changed either. We can't overcome what we don't resist. Disciples must unite together, anchored in the Word of God, confident in the Son of God, and led and empowered by the Spirit of God to resist and overcome just like their Master.

We can't overcome what we don't resist.

The Apostle John said that strength to resist and overcome was found in being rooted and remaining in the Word of God. (❏ Read 1 John 2:14.) The Apostle Paul wrote that being clothed and covered in the armor of God would enable us to stand strong against every scheme of hell. (❏ Read Ephesians 6:10-17.) Included in this is using the Word of God as the sword of the Spirit to cut through every lie and conquer through the light of

Notes

divine revelation. Led by the Spirit, we must resist and overcome every enemy and temptation by speaking the truth of God's Word in faith-filled confidence and clarity.

Throughout the New Testament and all of church history Jesus' followers resisted and overcame the ways of the world, the work of the flesh, and the wiles of the devil by the truth of the Word and the person and power of the Holy Spirit. What was true for them is true for us as well. Victory and freedom are the promised possessions of all who choose to live in the liberating life of Jesus. (❏ Read Revelation 12:11.)

MEMORIZE: *"You are of God, little children, and have overcome them, because He who is in you is greater than he who is in the world."* (1 John 4:4)

Use the following lines to write out the scripture to help you commit it to memory.

_____

_____

_____

_____

_____

_____

_____

KEY TRUTH: Disciples must unite together, anchored in the Word of God, confident in the Son of God, and led and empowered by the Spirit of God to resist and overcome just like their Master.

YOUR RESPONSE:

This is how you can respond in loving obedience to Jesus as you apply the truths from this lesson to your life.

- Ask the Holy Spirit to show you what represents resistance and temptation from the world, the flesh, and the devil in this season of your life.

- Ask the Holy Spirit to show you scriptures to memorize and with which to arm yourself.

- Led by the Spirit, pray these scriptures out in faith whenever faced with resistance and/or temptation.

- Find a group of disciples who will partner with you in resisting and overcoming.

WRITTEN RESPONSE: LESSON REVIEW

Review each section from the lesson on the previous pages to fill in each blank below. This review will help to reinforce the truths from this lesson in your life.

1. The word _____ in this verse means to vigorously _____, bravely _____, _____ face-to-face against an adversary, and _____ your ground.

2. The Bible tells us that we _____ the world through our _____ in the _____ and _____ of Jesus Christ.

3. Throughout Jesus' _____, we see Him using the _____ of God's _____ as His primary _____.

4. The Apostle Paul taught the _____ that _____ and _____ is the _____ and _____ of all disciples.

5. Disciples must _____ together, _____ in the Word of God, _____ in the Son of God, and _____ and _____ by the Spirit of God to _____ and _____ just like their Master.

WRITTEN RESPONSE: LIFE REFLECTION

Using the journaling section on the pages at the end of this lesson, write in your own words your responses to the following questions.

1. What have your learned and what has impacted you personally from this lesson?

2. In reading the scripture references in this lesson, what are you sensing and seeing the Holy Spirit highlighting and revealing to you that will enable you to better follow Jesus?

3. As a disciple and follower of Jesus, what steps of loving obedience do you need to take to see what you have learned in this lesson become ongoing practices and patterns in your life?

Journal

Journal

Journal

—

FOLLOWING JESUS IN SERVING AND GIVING

SERVING AND GIVING INTRODUCTION

❏ *Read Mark 10:42-45*

Near the end of Jesus' earthly ministry, He found it necessary to sum up for His disciples how to steward well the resources and relationships entrusted to them. They were looking for what gain and glory they might receive personally through their connection to Him. But He wanted them to understand that whatever had been given to them was to be used as kingdom currency to serve sacrificially and give generously for the purpose of redeeming, reconciling and restoring people. Jesus' message to them was that even He, their Messiah and Master, did not come to use position, possessions or power as a means to be served or catered to, but rather as a means to minister to the needs of others. Jesus saw His life as a ransom offering to be given unreservedly to serve and save bound and broken people everywhere. The word *ransom* means the payment or price given to free one from slavery or captivity. Jesus came to give life and liberty to all, releasing them from bondage to sin and death. (❏ Read Luke 4:18-19.) Our Lord paid the highest price and gave everything He had to serve mankind's deepest needs for God's greatest glory—He intended for His followers to do the same.

Jesus made it clear that everything we have of value is to be secured to souls and linked to lives. (❏ Read Mark

Jesus made it clear that everything we have of value is to be secured to souls and linked to lives.

10:17-21; Luke 22:24-30.) According to Jesus, all the resources we have been given to steward are to be used for the serving of and giving to others. (❏ Luke 12:31-34.) We have been called to mark and measure our real riches and truest treasures—our relationships with precious people in the church and the world. Serving and giving are two sides of the same kingdom coin.

SERVING AND GIVING DEFINED

In the Scriptures, *serving* means meeting spiritual and physical needs and making a positive difference in the lives of others. Serving has to do with anything and everything that helps and heals the human condition. To define, describe and illustrate serving in the clearest way possible, Jesus got down on His hands and knees and washed the feet of His disciples. (❏ Read John 13:12-17.) In so doing, He declared to them that the exercising of kingdom authority was not done with a scepter, but a basin and a towel. He also declared that serving was, in fact, the only real and true greatness in His kingdom. (❏ Read Matthew 20:26-28.)

In the Scriptures, *giving* means presenting tithes, offerings and charitable gifts—or anything of value in one's life and possessions—to honor God and to bless others. (❑ Read Malachi 3:10-12; Matthew 6:1-4; Acts 20:32-35.) Giving is to be done with generosity of heart and hands. (❑ Read 2 Corinthians 9:6-7.) It is to be abundantly sown in faith as one believes that a harvest of resources to be reaped and further released. Giving includes time, talent and treasure, offered generously and intentionally for righteous and redemptive purposes. (❑ Read Proverbs 3:9-10; 11:24-26.)

SERVING AND GIVING IN THE LIFE OF JESUS

Jesus' entire earthly life and ministry was a picture and a pattern of serving and giving sacrificially and generously for redemptive purposes. (❑ Read Matthew 20:27-28.) In His coming to earth, He came as an act of serving and giving on the part of the Father, who gave the treasure of heaven to serve and save the inhabitants of earth. (❑ Read John 3:16-17; Romans 8:31-32; 1 Corinthians 2:12.) Jesus taught that obeying the command to serve and give generously would result in the release of a return from God that would

To Jesus, everything He said and everything He did was about helping people rightly relate to God and rightly relate to one another.

be abundant and overflowing. (❏ Read Luke 6:38.)

In all of Jesus' message and ministry concerning serving and giving, He linked the stewarding of resources with the stewarding of relationships. (❏ Matthew 23:23; Mark 14:3-9; Luke 7:44-48.) To Jesus, everything He said and everything He did was about helping people rightly relate to God and rightly relate to one another. Serving and giving were always attached to resourcing people's lives with all they needed, spiritually, physically and materially to become fully what God the Father and Jesus the Son intended them to be. This must be the example we follow in serving with our time, talent and treasure and the giving of our tithes, offerings and charitable gifts. In our serving and giving, as with Jesus, everything must be secured to souls and linked to lives.

SERVING AND GIVING
IN THE LIVES OF JESUS' FOLLOWERS

Jesus' followers learned well how to live lives of serving and giving. The Lord pointed and paved the way that was theirs to follow. Jesus' disciples gave up all they possessed to serve the Master and follow Him into a process of becoming fishers of men who transformed lives and changed nations. (❏ Read Luke 5:9-11; Matthew 28:18-20.) Jesus promised them that if they gave all to serve all, they would be rewarded with abundant resources to meet their needs to continue in serving and giving to

others. (❏ Read Mark 10:28-30; Luke 18:28-30.) The
Apostle Paul told the elders of the church at Ephesus
that he had modeled for them how to steward resources
and relationships in serving and giving sacrificially and
joyfully. (❏ Read Acts 20:32-34.) In fact, he reminded
them of the words of Jesus when He said, "It is more
blessed to give than to receive." (❏ Read Acts 20:35.) The
Apostle Peter instructed his readers that any spiritual gift
or grace given by God was to be released in service to the
people He puts in one's life. (❏ Read 1 Peter 4:10-11.) He
told them they were to be faithful stewards of every good
thing that had been divinely deposited into their lives.
The writer of Hebrews sums up serving and giving well
as sacrifices offered to a God who is well-pleased, and to
others who are well-served. (❏ Read Hebrews 13:16.)

In all these examples and many more, these followers of
Jesus revealed their commitment to steward resources and
relationships through their serving and giving. They saw
all of their time, talent and treasure as divine provision
to be managed well that they might minister well. They
understood that their only true success was found in souls
saved and disciples made, and they used everything they
had received to be everything they released unto that end.

SERVING AND GIVING
IN OUR LIVES

As it was for Jesus' followers, so it must be for us with what we possess from God's gracious hand. Time, talent and treasure—and tithes, offerings and charitable gifts—are the resources we must steward in serving and giving. Brothers and sisters, neighbors and nations are the relationships we must steward in serving and giving. We must always see these things as interconnected to one another. As stated earlier in this lesson, we must see everything we have and everything we do as secured to souls and linked to lives. All of our *serving* must have people's lives and eternal destinies in view. All of our *giving* must have people's lives and eternal destinies in view. For when the personal lives of precious people who God loves deeply are our focus, our serving and giving will rise to unprecedented levels of abundance and excellence.

... we must see everything we have and everything we do as secured to souls and linked to lives.

MEMORIZE: *"For even the Son of Man did not come to be served, but to serve, and to give His life a ransom for many."* (Mark 10:45)

Use the following lines to write out the scripture to help you commit it to memory.

_____

_____

_____

_____

_____

_____

_____

KEY TRUTH: Jesus' entire earthly life and ministry was a picture and a pattern of serving and giving sacrificially and generously for redemptive purposes.

YOUR RESPONSE:

This is how you can respond in loving obedience to Jesus as you apply the truths from this lesson to your life.

- Freshly surrender your time, talent and treasure to Jesus, acknowledging that everything belongs to Him and that you are to be a faithful steward of it all.

- Make sure that with the financial resources entrusted to you, there is the setting aside of the tithes, offerings and charitable gifts to honor God as creator and provider and to bless and build up others.

- Ask the Holy Spirit to reveal to you whether or not all of your serving and giving is secured to souls and linked to lives, enabling you to steward, connect and integrate resources and relationships.

- Make a list of the people Jesus has called you to serve and give your life for redemptive purposes and pray daily for them as brothers and sisters, neighbors and nations.

WRITTEN RESPONSE: LESSON REVIEW

Review each section from the lesson on the previous pages to fill in each blank below. This review will help to reinforce the truths from this lesson in your life.

1. In the Scriptures, _____ means meeting
    _____ and _____ needs and making a
    _____ _____ in the lives of others.

2. In the Scriptures, _____ means presenting tithes,
    offerings and charitable gifts—or anything of _____
    in one's _____ and _____ —to
    _____ God and to _____ others.

3. Jesus' entire earthly _____ and
    _____ was a _____ and a
    _____ of serving and giving _____
    and _____ for redemptive purposes.

4. In all these examples and many more, these _____
    of Jesus _____ their _____ to
    steward _____ and _____ through
    their _____ and _____.

5. As stated earlier in this lesson, we must see _____
    we have and _____ we do as _____ to
    _____ and _____ to _____.

WRITTEN RESPONSE: LIFE REFLECTION

Using the journaling section on the pages at the end of this lesson,
write in your own words your responses to the following questions.

1. What have your learned and what has impacted you personally
    from this lesson?

2. In reading the scripture references in this lesson, what are you
    sensing and seeing the Holy Spirit highlighting and revealing to
    you that will enable you to better follow Jesus?

3. As a disciple and follower of Jesus, what steps of loving
    obedience do you need to take to see what you have learned in
    this lesson become ongoing practices and patterns in your life?

Journal

Journal

Lesson 11

———

FOLLOWING JESUS IN SACRIFICING AND SUFFERING

SACRIFICING AND SUFFERING INTRODUCTION

❏ *Read Philippians 2:5-11*

When Jesus took on human flesh, He made the greatest sacrifice and paid the greatest price that anyone had ever offered. And when Jesus took on human flesh, He suffered the greatest pain and endured the greatest trials anyone had ever experienced. In His sacrifice, He stepped out of eternity and into time, out of heaven and onto earth and out of spirit and into flesh. He humbly and willingly made every sacrifice to provide the greatest offering for the blessing and benefit of all. In His suffering, He endured every possible pain, persecution and redemptive process, including and especially laying down His life in death, as He hung His sinless life on a sinner's cross. Jesus saw all of His sacrificing and suffering as necessary to bring glory to God and good to others.

The Apostle Paul told the Philippians that Jesus' mindset and ministry, attitudes and actions, were to be theirs as well. He told them no price was too great to pay in order to serve God and others, and no amount of suffering was too much to bear if it meant furthering the message and ministry of the gospel of Christ Jesus in the church

> *Jesus saw all of His sacrificing and suffering as necessary to bring glory to God and good to others.*

and the world. (❑ Read Philippians 1:27-30; 2:1-4, 14-18.) What was true for them is true for us as well. We must, by God's sustaining and strengthening grace, live lives of sacrificing and suffering when necessary to follow the extravagant example of Jesus our Lord.

SACRIFICING AND SUFFERING DEFINED

In the Scriptures, *sacrificing* is paying any price and going to any length for whatever produces God's highest glory and people's highest good. A *sacrifice* was something offered up, and something offered for a sacred and holy purpose. In the Old Testament, it was the lives of bulls and goats and rams and lambs whose blood was shed as a sacred offering to cover sin and honor a holy God. (❑ Read Hebrews 9:19-22.) In the New Testament, it was the ultimate sacrifice made and the ultimate price paid through the shed blood of Jesus Christ. (❑ Read Hebrews 9:23-28.) Then, it was the sacred offering of His disciples and followers as they laid their lives down, going to any length to love Christ and love others completely. (❑ Read John 15:12-13; 2 Timothy 4:6-7.)

In the Scriptures, *suffering* is enduring any pain, persecution or demanding process for a greater and godly purpose. (❑ Read 1 Peter 3:13-17.) The pain can be physical, mental or emotional. (❑ Read 2 Corinthians 12:7-10.) The persecution is the result of the ungodly and wicked resisting the efforts of the godly and righteous to honor God in word and deed. Most often, demonic entities are at work in fostering and fortifying the persecution. (❏ Read Ephesians 6:10-20.) The demanding process can have to do with anything that God takes one through to test, try and teach them, always unto greater faith and fruitfulness. In all suffering, it is God's will by God's work to bring His people through the suffering into fuller levels of growth and grace. (❏ Read James 1:2-4, 12-15.)

SACRIFICING AND SUFFERING IN THE LIFE OF JESUS

From beginning to end, Jesus' life was marked by sacrificing and suffering. His entrance into the human race was an unprecedented act of sacrifice. (❏ Read John 3:13-17.) From the beginning of His earthly ministry to the moment He said, "it is finished" while on the cross, Jesus sacrificed and suffered to seek and save a people lost and looking for hope. (❏ Read John 19:28-30.) He was heaven's Sacred Offering, offered up to a holy God and offered for a helpless people.

As God's perfect sacrifice, He suffered unto the shedding of blood and death on the cross to serve the deepest and most fundamental need of people everywhere and for all time. (❏ Read John 19:23-28.) And

> *... Jesus sacrificed and suffered to seek and save a people lost and looking for hope.*

when He was offered ways of escape from sacrificing and suffering, He resisted and refused, unwilling to compromise His calling to rescue, redeem and restore. (❑ Read Luke 4:1-13; Luke 23:36-39.) Even when offered something to deaden the agony of His physical pain while on the cross, He steadfastly refused. (❑ Read Matthew 27:23-34.) Jesus never sought to escape sacrificing and suffering. Instead, He embraced it, enduring temporary lack, shame and pain for the joy of serving and saving others. (❑ Read Hebrews 12:1-2.)

Jesus rose every day to live for others. There was no price He was unwilling to pay to meet the deepest places of human need. To Jesus, sacrificing and suffering were merely the cost of fulfilling His calling to declare and demonstrate the good news of God's love and power. And this is our calling as well—imitate the Master and His mission to lay one's life down that other's might be raised up and released into God's highest and fullest purpose for them.

SACRIFICING AND SUFFERING IN THE LIVES OF JESUS' FOLLOWERS

What Jesus initiated in sacrificing and suffering for the glory of God and the good of others, Jesus' followers imitated. Jesus' disciples left all to follow Him, sacrificing material and physical comfort and security for the sake of following the King and furthering the kingdom.

Notes

Notes

(❏ Read Mark 10:28-30; Luke 18:28-30.) In the early church, everyone was willing to make any sacrifice to meet every spiritual and physical need in their midst and in the community around them. (❏ Read Acts 2:44-45; 4:32-37.) The Apostle Paul both testified of His own willingness to sacrifice all for the cause of following Jesus, as well as commending Philippian believers for sacrificing resources and reputation to identify with him and his kingdom cause. (❏ Read Philippians 4:10-20.) In all these examples of sacrificing, there was the divine promise of divine provision for followers of Jesus who were willing to forsake all for the Master's mission.

... all suffering experienced according to the will of God will always be attended by the work of God's grace, enabling all to endure victoriously.

When Jesus' disciples, Peter and John, were unfairly tried and severely persecuted by the religious leaders of the day, they stood their ground by the grace and power of the Holy Spirit and gave faithful witness to their Lord. After suffering a verbal attack and a vicious beating, they were released. Their response to all of this was stunning. Rather than retreat in fear, they rejoiced in faith for the privilege of suffering pain and shame for the name of Jesus. (❏ Read Acts 5:27-32, 40-42.) The Apostle Paul, already suffering in Roman imprisonment

for his faith, wrote to the same Philippian believers that he
considered their suffering, and his, to be proof of allegiance
to Jesus and a process and pathway to know Him more
deeply and make Him known. (❑ Read Philippians 1:27-30;
3:7-11.) In the Scriptures, and throughout history, Jesus'
followers have discovered that all suffering experienced
according to the will of God will always be attended by the
work of God's grace, enabling all to endure victoriously.

SACRIFICING AND SUFFERING IN OUR LIVES

Now it is our time and our turn to pay any price and
endure any pain, persecution or process for a greater and
godly purpose. Sacrificing and suffering are to be acts
of devoted worship to the Living God. (❑ Read Romans
12:1-2.) While it may seem that sacrificing and suffering
will make our lives less meaningful and fulfilling, the exact
opposite is true. For it is in sacrificing and suffering for
the eternal purposes of God the Father through Jesus the
Son that we find our true identity and purpose. Sacrificing
and suffering are a pathway and a process with profound
promise—growth and blessing spiritually, relationally,
missionally and materially. (❑ Read Matthew 19:27-30.)

The sacrificing is worth whatever price we pay because
each sacrifice is made to make precious people true sons
and daughters of Father God, and true followers and
disciples of the Lord Jesus. Sacrificing is our lives being

Notes

offered up to our worthy God and being offered for a waiting world. The suffering is worth whatever pain, persecution of demanding processes we go through because it is working a greater and eternal weight of glory in our lives and the lives of all we touch. (❏ Read 2 Corinthians 4:16-18.) Suffering is our lives being tested and tried to make us stronger in faith and deeper in Christ.

Sacrificing and suffering are to be acts of devoted worship to the Living God.

MEMORIZE: *"Beloved, do not think it strange concerning the fiery trial which is to try you, as though some strange thing happened to you; but rejoice to the extent that you partake of Christ's sufferings, that when His glory is revealed, you may also be glad with exceeding joy."* (1 Peter 4:12-13)

Use the following lines to write out the scripture to help you commit it to memory.

_____

_____

_____

_____

_____

_____

_____

KEY TRUTH: What Jesus initiated in sacrificing and suffering for the glory of God and the good of others, Jesus' followers imitated.

YOUR RESPONSE:

This is how you can respond in loving obedience to Jesus as you apply the truths from this lesson to your life.

- Ask the Holy Spirit to reveal any areas in your life that you need to let go and lay down in complete sacrifice for the purposes and plans of God.

- Ask the Holy Spirit to help strengthen you to embrace and endure pain, persecution and demanding processes, believing that suffering according to the will of God will produce growth and depth in your life.

- Review situations and seasons in your life where you made significant sacrifices and came through times of suffering that produced greater blessing and boldness.

- Make a fresh and faith-filled confession and commitment to pay any price and endure any pain, by God's grace, to advance God's purposes.

WRITTEN RESPONSE: LESSON REVIEW

Review each section from the lesson on the previous pages to fill in each blank below. This review will help to reinforce the truths from this lesson in your life.

1. In the Scriptures, _____ is paying any

   _____ and going to any _____ for

   whatever _____ God's highest _____

   and people's highest _____.

2. In the Scriptures, _____ is enduring

   any _____, _____ or

   demanding _____ for a _____

   and _____ purpose.

3. To Jesus, _____ and _____

   were merely the cost of _____ His calling to

   _____ and _____ the good news

   of God's _____ and _____.

4. Jesus' disciples left _____ to _____

   Him, _____ material and physical _____

   and _____ for the sake of _____

   the King and _____ the kingdom.

5. Sacrificing and suffering are a _____

   and a _____ with _____

   _____ – growth and blessing _____,

   _____, _____ and _____.

WRITTEN RESPONSE: LIFE REFLECTION

Using the journaling section on the pages at the end of this lesson, write in your own words your responses to the following questions.

1. What have your learned and what has impacted you personally from this lesson?

2. In reading the scripture references in this lesson, what are you sensing and seeing the Holy Spirit highlighting and revealing to you that will enable you to better follow Jesus?

3. As a disciple and follower of Jesus, what steps of loving obedience do you need to take to see what you have learned in this lesson become ongoing practices and patterns in your life?

Journal

Journal

Journal

FOLLOWING JESUS IN RESTING AND ABIDING

Notes

RESTING AND ABIDING INTRODUCTION

❏ *Read Matthew 11:28-30*

Throughout the Bible there are promises of rest and peace for the people of God. Jesus came to earth during a weary and restless time in Israel's history. The religious leaders had made all attempts at living for God burdensome. They put heavy laws and countless rules on the people. The scribes and Pharisees added to the Word of God and required the people to obey traditions rather than scriptural truths. In the eyes of these religious leaders, the more rules you attempted to follow, the more respected you were. It became a contest to see who could do the most rule-following in their own strength. The problem, though, was that no one was getting any closer to an intimate relationship with God, and everyone was growing tired of trying.

Jesus showed people how one could abound in strength, endurance, and rest while diligently doing the work of the kingdom.

Then Jesus came modeling an abiding relationship with God the Father. Jesus was full of joy, full of peace, and full of strength. He and He alone offered the key to a life of rest found through an abiding relationship with the Living God. Jesus called out to the multitudes of tired, joyless, frustrated and hopeless people inviting them to come to Him and discover a reprieve for their restless souls. To those who responded to that call, He showed them how to live a life of resting while working with God. Jesus showed people how one could abound in strength, endurance, and rest while diligently doing the work of the kingdom. As time went on, His disciples learned to follow His example. The good news for them, and for followers of Jesus for all time, was that real resting could be found through authentic abiding in Him.

RESTING AND ABIDING DEFINED

Jesus called those who labored and were heavy laden to come to Him and find rest. (❑ Read Matthew 11:28.) The word *labor* in this verse has to do with working in your own strength. The term *heavy laden* has to do with carrying burdens put on you by another. The word for *resting* in the Scriptures means being given permission to stop. Jesus gives every disciple the permission to stop working in their own strength and carrying burdens put on them by others, and not by Him.

Just as Jesus did nothing apart from the will of His Father and the work of the Holy Spirit, so we are called to do nothing apart from Him.

The word for *abiding* in the New Testament has to do with attaching and remaining—not detaching nor departing—holding onto something, continuing and enduring in something. Christ's abiding relationship with the Father becomes the model for our abiding relationship with Him. Just as Jesus did nothing apart from the will of His Father and the work of the Holy Spirit, so we are called to do nothing apart from Him. It is this abiding relationship with Him that provides the abiding rest in Him. (❏ Read John 15:4-10.)

RESTING AND ABIDING IN THE LIFE OF JESUS

Jesus exemplified physical rest and refreshment, and spiritual, mental, and emotional peace. We have no record in the Bible of Jesus ever being anxious. We have no record of Jesus ever being so emotionally exhausted that He was unable to fulfill the Father's will. Jesus was full of peace and joy and told His disciples that as they abided in Him, their peace and joy would be full as well. (❏ Read John 15:11.) It was Christ's moment-by-moment intimacy with and dependence upon the Father that kept Him serene and confident. Jesus lived in abundant joy, perpetual inner pleasure, and relentless

> *Jesus exemplified physical rest and refreshment, and spiritual, mental, and emotional peace.*

rest because He abided in the presence of His Father
through the Holy Spirit. (❏ Read Psalm 16:11.)

Right before Jesus' crucifixion He told His disciples that
He was granting them the gift of divine peace through
the Holy Spirit, who He would send to be the source
of His life in them. He told them they had no reason
to fear, and no reason for their hearts to be troubled
or overly concerned. He told them by abiding in Him
as He had abided in the Father, they would experience
and express the same undisturbed composure that
they had seen manifested in Him. Rest and renewal
would be their perpetual state as they stayed constantly
connected to Him. (❏ Read John 14:25-27; 15:9-11.)

RESTING AND ABIDING
IN THE LIVES OF JESUS' FOLLOWERS

Jesus' disciples learned to follow His example by resting
and abiding in Him. They learned that their primary
need was not rest *from* work, but rather rest *in* work –
the work He had called them to. As they went out and
preached everywhere, the Lord Jesus worked alongside
them confirming their message with mighty signs and
wonders. (❏ Read Mark 16:20.) It was in their abiding
in Him that they found their anointing through Him,
which provided the perpetual rest that was in and of Him.
The early church found this same deep refreshment and
rest as they lived life in Jesus together. (❏ Read Acts

2:46.) By yoking up with Jesus, these disciples carried no unnecessary burdens. They lived in a constant state of gladness and singleness of heart and purpose.

The Apostle Paul often began his letters to the churches with a greeting of grace, peace and rest found in an abiding relationship with God the Father and the Lord Jesus Christ. (❑ Read 2 Corinthians 1:1-2.) This same Paul wrote that while believers' lives in the flesh were frail and limited, they were filled with the extraordinary power and strength of God. (❑ Read 2 Corinthians 4:7.) He likened believers' lives to clay pots – fragile and easily broken. Yet, at the same time, he wrote that while the human vessel was vulnerable, it could also be made victorious and powerful through the inner work of God's grace. Paul's testimony was that throughout his life of resting and abiding in Christ Jesus, he found the strength he needed to declare the gospel and to demonstrate its love and power. (❑ Read 2 Timothy 4:17.)

Living abiding in the life-giving will and work of our Lord will always produce encouragement and effectiveness.

RESTING AND ABIDING
IN OUR LIVES

We are a natural people living with and linked to a supernatural Savior. And while our bodies will experience fatigue and tire, our souls can experience a state of perpetual refreshment. This was Jesus' promise to His original followers and is His promise to us as His followers as well. (❑ Read Isaiah 54:13; Matthew 11:28-30.) The key to this is always the same – remain yoked to Jesus, abiding in a relationship of rest and renewal in Him. Living apart from the life-giving will and work of our Lord will always produce frustration and failure. Living abiding in the life-giving will and work of our Lord will always produce encouragement and effectiveness.

The Lord who calls His disciples into the yoke to work is also the Good Shepherd who causes His sheep to lie down in green pastures. (❑ Read Psalm 23:1-2.) The Lord who calls us each morning to rise from our bed is the same Lord who calls us each evening to lie down and sleep peacefully. (❑ Read Psalm 4:8; Psalm 127:2.) Jesus does not make His disciples weary and heavy laden. He doesn't overload them, He doesn't overwork them, and He doesn't overwhelm them. Instead, He strengthens, sustains and refreshes all who pursue resting and abiding in Him.

MEMORIZE: *"Come to Me, all you who labor and are heavy laden, and I will give you rest. Take My yoke upon you and learn from Me, for I am gentle and lowly in heart, and you will find rest for your souls. For My yoke is easy and My burden is light."*
(Matthew 11:28-30)

Use the following lines to write out the scripture to help you commit it to memory.

_____

_____

_____

_____

_____

_____

KEY TRUTH: Just as Jesus did nothing apart from the will of His Father and the work of the Holy Spirit, so we are called to do nothing apart from Him. It is this abiding relationship with Him that provides the abiding rest in Him.

YOUR RESPONSE:

This is how you can respond in loving obedience to Jesus as you apply the truths from this lesson to your life.

- Ask the Holy Spirit to show you any situations in your life where you walk in your own strength.

- Ask the Holy Spirit to show you any attitudes, actions, and/or responsibilities that are keeping you from resting and abiding.

- Ask the Holy Spirit to show you specific areas where you must grow in endurance for the assignments the Lord is giving you as you rest and abide.

- Commit to Jesus that you will abide in Him and walk in His strength for His work.

WRITTEN RESPONSE: LESSON REVIEW

Review each section from the lesson on the previous pages to fill in each blank below. This review will help to reinforce the truths from this lesson in your life.

1. The word for _____ in the Scriptures means being _____ _____ to _____.

2. The word for _____ in the New Testament has to do with _____ and _____ —not detaching nor departing—_____ onto something, _____ and _____ in something.

3. Jesus lived in abundant _____, perpetual inner _____, and relentless _____ because He _____ in the _____ of His Father through the Holy Spirit.

4. Jesus' _____ learned to _____ His example by _____ and _____ in Him.

5. Living _____ from the life-giving _____ and _____ of our Lord will always produce _____ and _____.

WRITTEN RESPONSE: LIFE REFLECTION

Using the journaling section on the pages at the end of this lesson,
write in your own words your responses to the following questions.

1. What have your learned and what has impacted you personally
    from this lesson?

2. In reading the scripture references in this lesson, what are you
    sensing and seeing the Holy Spirit highlighting and revealing to
    you that will enable you to better follow Jesus?

3. As a disciple and follower of Jesus, what steps of loving
    obedience do you need to take to see what you have learned in
    this lesson become ongoing practices and patterns in your life?

Journal

Journal

Journal

Journal

Journal

Journal

Journal

Journal

Journal

Journal

Journal

Made in the
USA
Middletown, DE